"Would you Rather?" For Kids

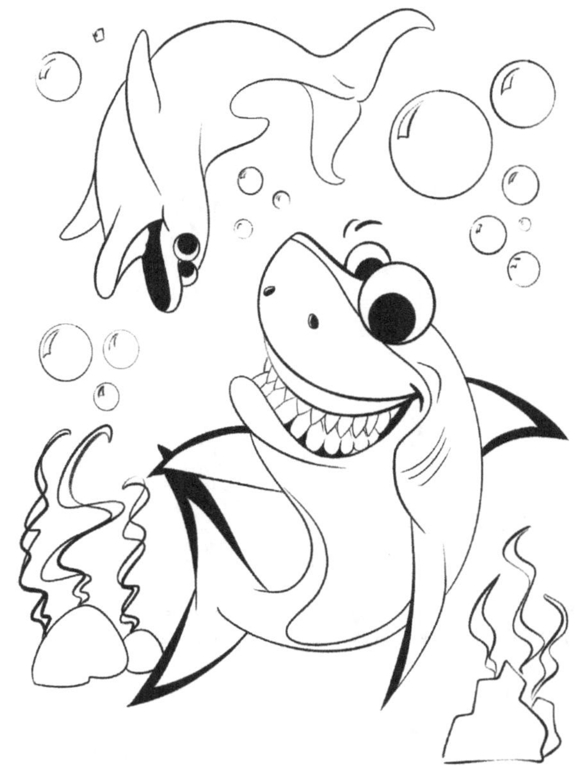

Laugh Out Loud With Fun Questions
And Silly Scenarios For Kids!

By Charlotte Gibbs

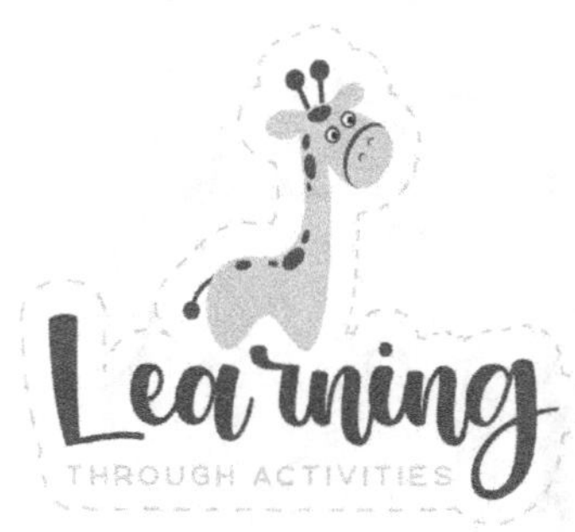

WOULd you RATHeR?

SPECIAL BONUS!

Want These 2 Books For <u>FREE</u>?

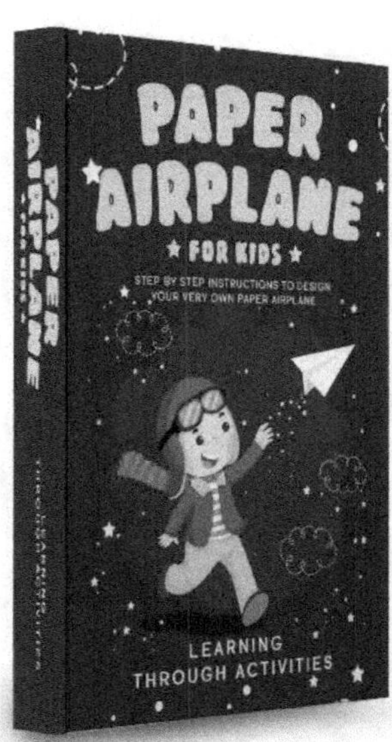

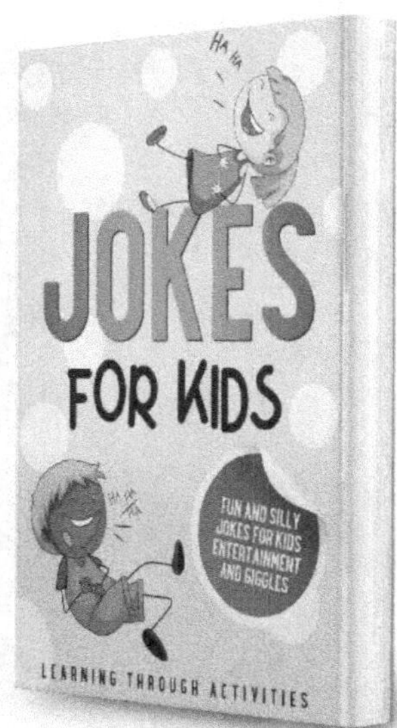

Get <u>FREE</u>, unlimited access to these and all of our new kids books by joining our community!

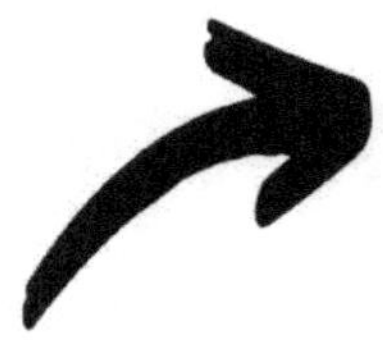

Scan W/ Your Camera To Join!

Table of Contents

Introduction

Choo-choo! All aboard the "Would you Rather" train! In this game, you'll have to make some tough — and silly — calls between two fun situations.

Some of the questions might make you laugh, gasp, or think really hard, but I promise you that they'll be fun. You might even learn something about yourself and the people around you along the way!

Are you interested in dancing with monkeys on Mars or would you rather walk along the rings of Saturn? These kinds of questions will be asked in the following pages and you'll be able to answer them with your friends, family, and relatives. Remember to ask "Why?" Why would you rather dance with monkeys? Because they're fun, cute, or silly? The answer you give can teach everyone a thing or two about your personality — especially when it comes time to explain why.

Remember to read each question carefully and pick the answer that best fits who you are! It's simple and exciting to answer these questions, especially when in a group.

The rule of the game is easy: pick one or the other. Choosing neither or both is not an option! It's okay to be torn between the answers, but you have to pick a side eventually. Raise the stakes by setting a timer if you'd like! Doing a speedy game of "Would You Rather" can also be fun and exciting.

Act out the situations, make up dances about the options , or create stories about the questions if that makes you happy.

The point is to have fun!

Get ready. Get set. Enjoy!

Chapter One: Would You Rather?

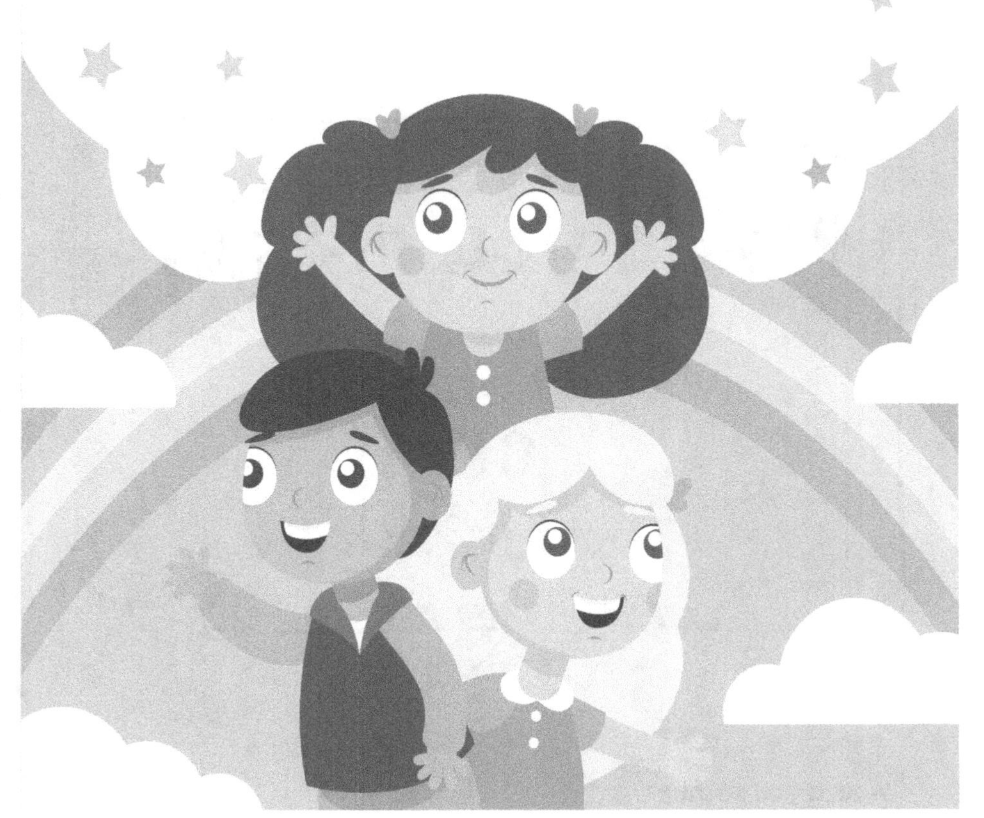

Would you rather

jump on clouds
or
swim in Jell-O?

Would you rather

be a wizard
or
be a lizard?

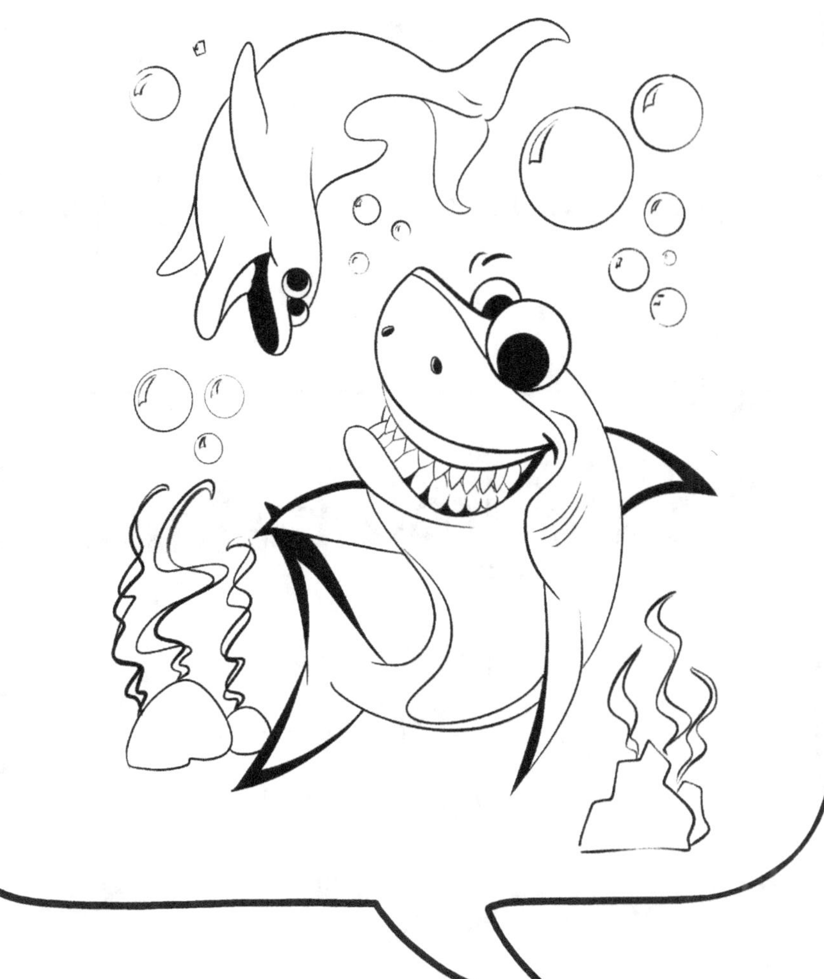

Would you rather

be a shark **or** be a dolphin?

Would you rather

stop time
or
travel in time?

Would you rather

have one eye
or
one hundred eyes?

Would you rather

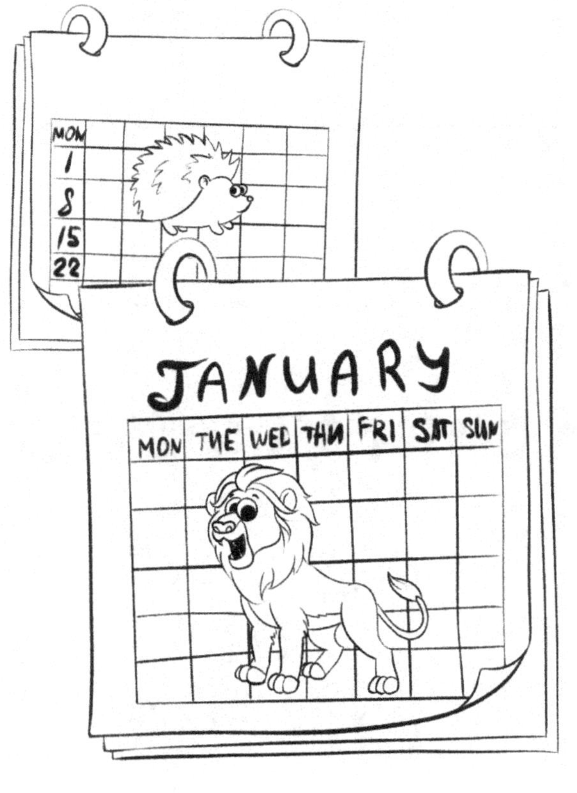

Would you rather

have a pet robot
or
have a pet koala?

Would you rather

visit Antarctica
or
visit Africa?

Would you rather

be able to talk to dogs and cats
or

read human minds?

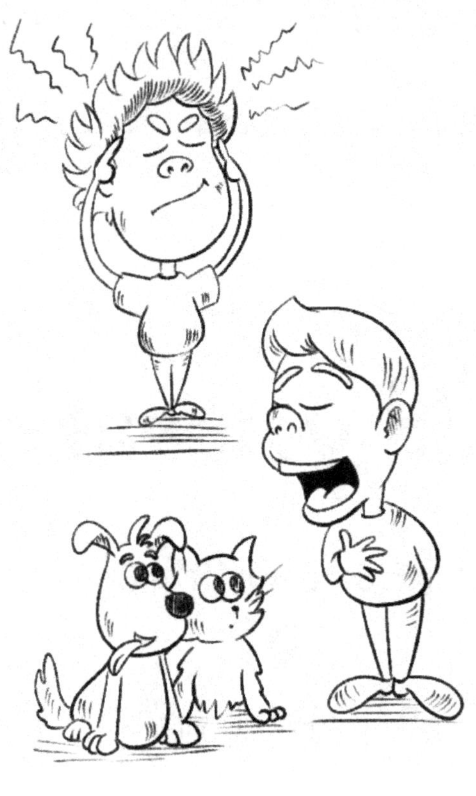

Would you rather

have a tornado for a teacher
or
have an elephant for a principal?

Would you rather

be a famous pirate
or
be a famous artist?

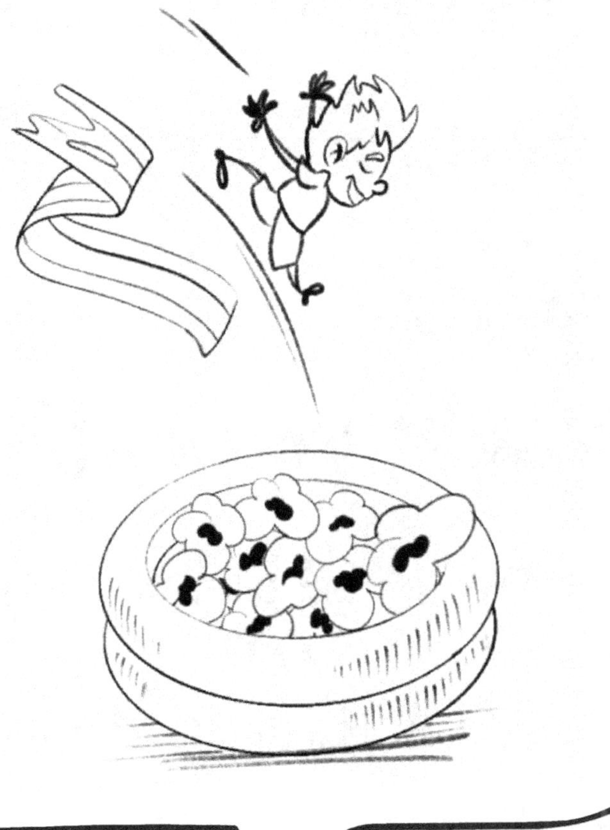

Would you rather

swim in a pool of popcorn
or
run on a road of bubblegum?

Would you rather

have wings like a hummingbird
or
have scales like a tuna fish?

Would you rather

have one big birthday party
or
have ten small birthday parties a year?

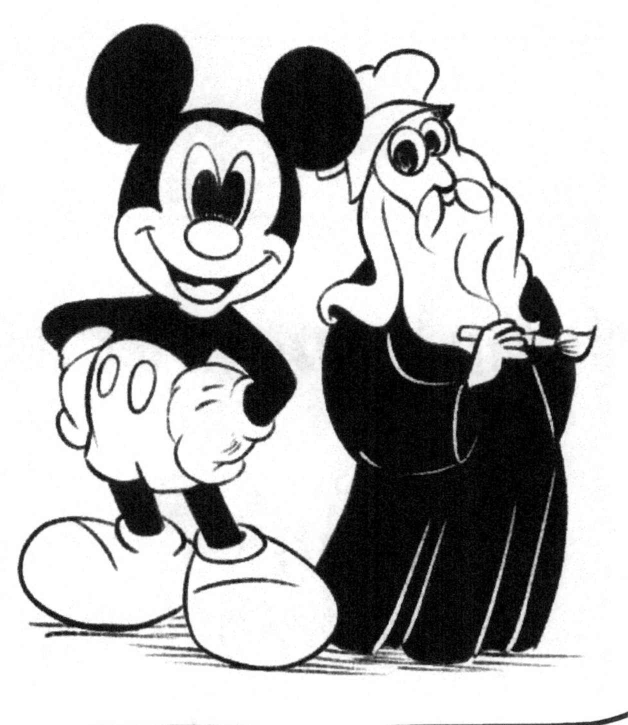

Would you rather

meet Mickey Mouse
or
meet Leonardo da Vinci?

Would you rather
drink chocolate milk for the rest
of your life
or
drink strawberry milk for the rest of
your life?

Would you rather
camp on the moon
or
collect rocks on mars?

Would you rather

hike in the jungle
or
ride a camel in the desert?

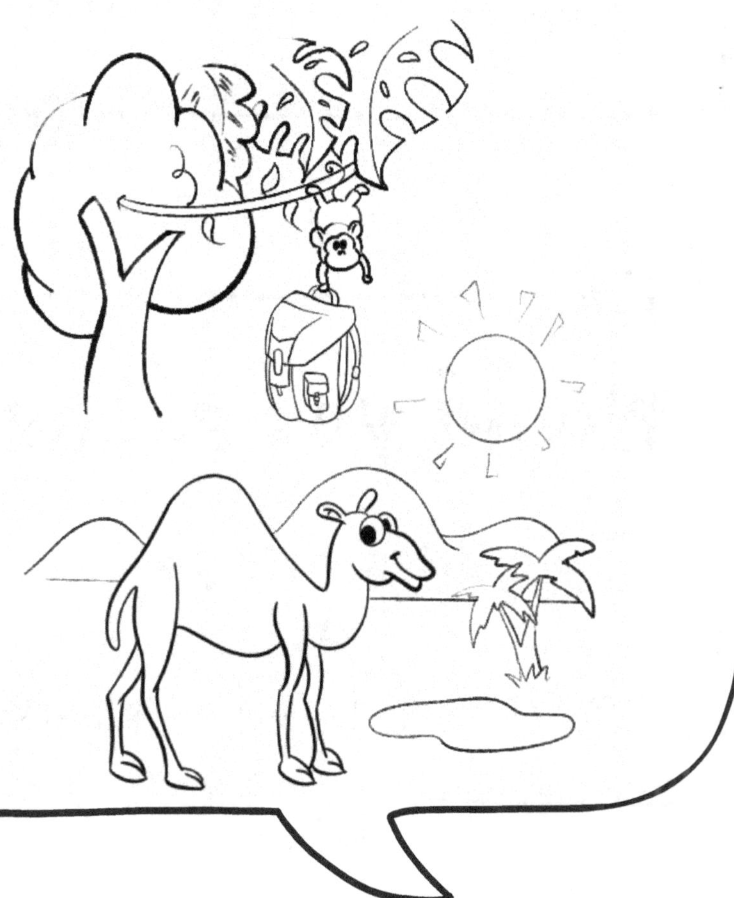

Would you rather

sleep upside down like a bat
or
sleep standing up like a horse?

Would you rather

dye your hair pink
or
grow your hair twenty more inches?

Would you rather

make rainbow cupcakes
or
peanut butter brownies?

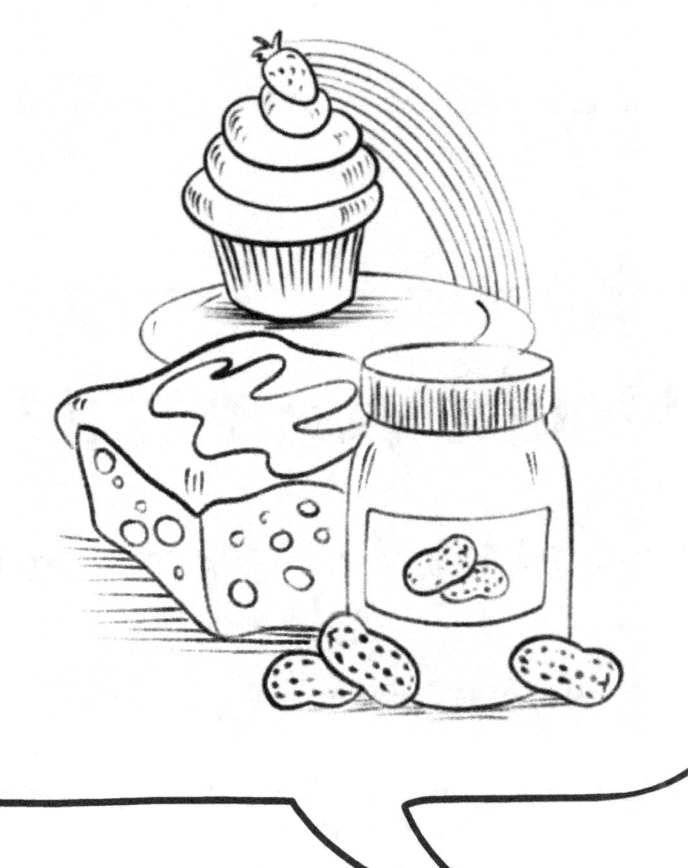

Would you rather

go skiing in snowy mountains
or
go surfing in crystal clear oceans?

Would you rather

live in a dark cave during the winter
or
only eat broccoli all summer?

Would you rather

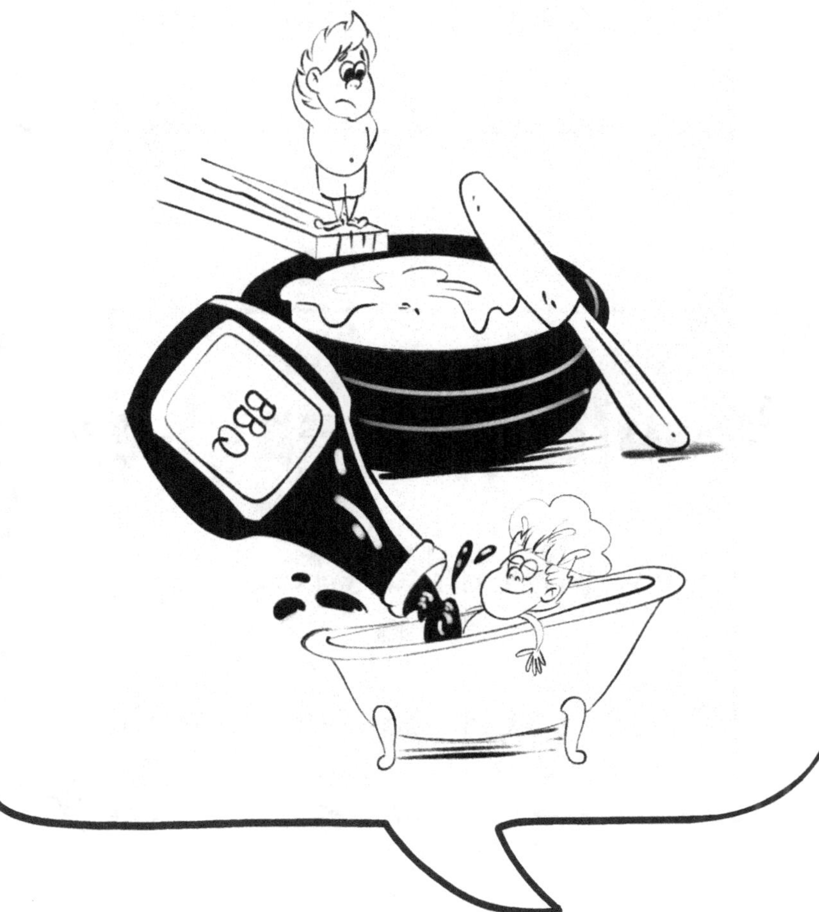

Would you rather

build your own treehouse
or
build your own blanket fort?

Would you rather

smell like a skunk for a day
or
be hairy like a bear for a month?

Would you rather

have lasers shoot from your eyes
or
flowers shoot from your nose?

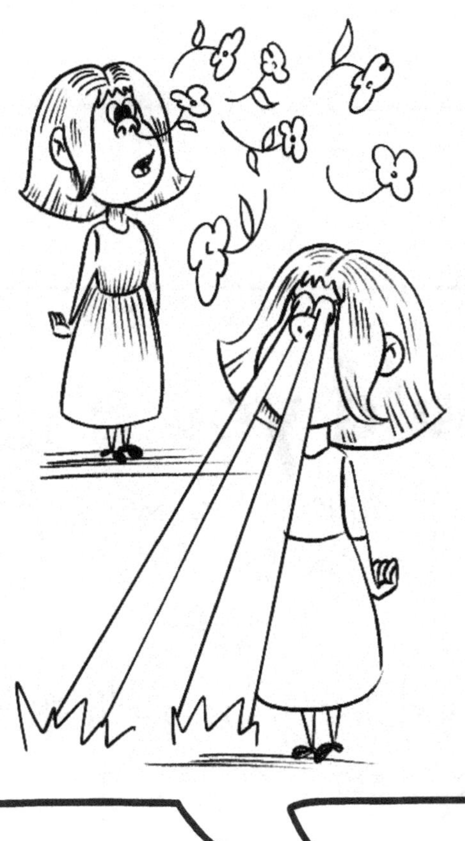

Would you rather

be able to breathe underwater
or
be able to breathe in space?

Would you rather

rather dance with monkeys on the
rings of Saturn
or
have dinner with yoda on Pluto?

Would you rather

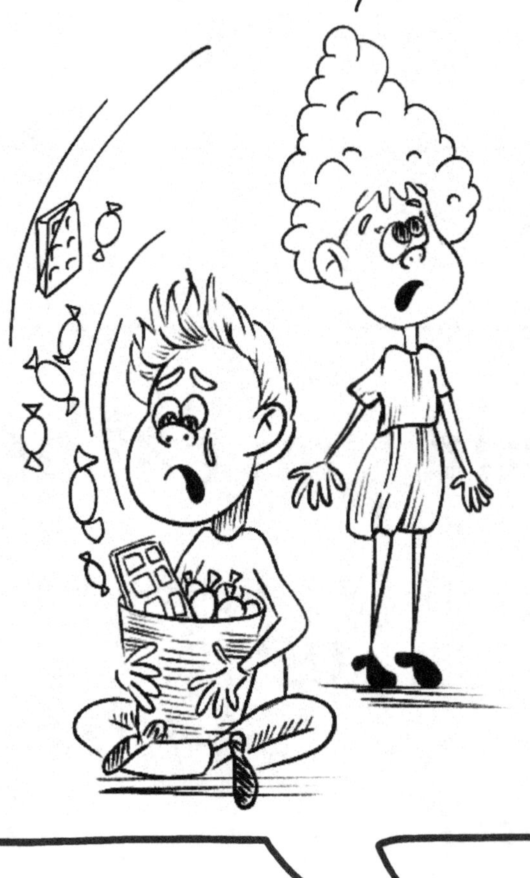

Would you rather

have baby feet
or
baby hands?

Would you rather

eat chicken nuggets made of Pop Rocks
or
pizza made of gummy bears?

Would you rather

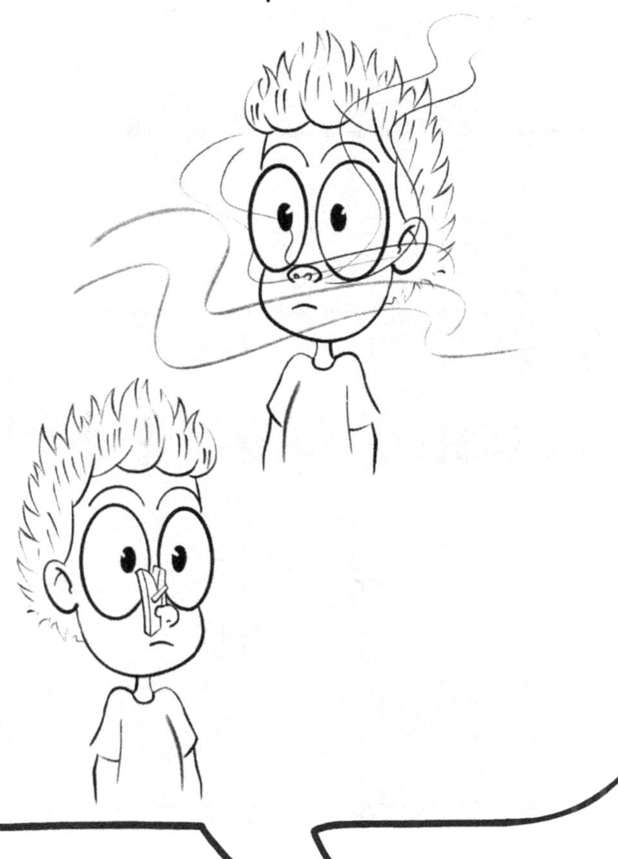

Would you rather

be the world's fastest swimmer
or
the world's best hockey player?

Would you rather

sing with Peter Pan
or
fly in the clouds with Taylor Swift?

Would you rather

have feet for hands
or
hands for feet?

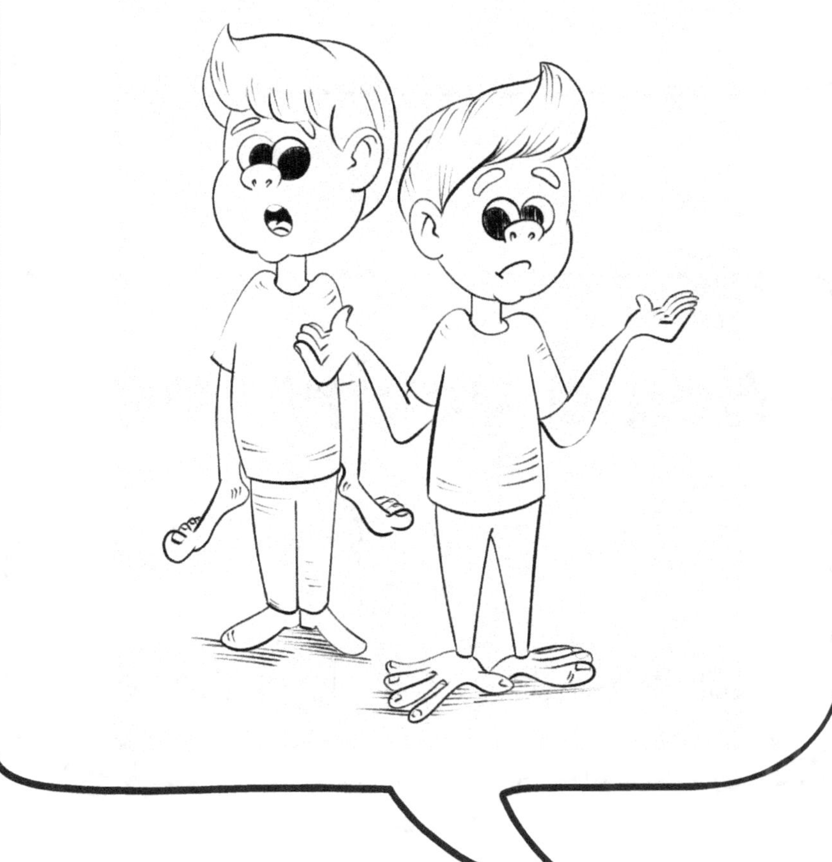

Would you rather

play with ten silly puppies
or
cuddle with ten playful kittens?

Would you rather

wear clown makeup to school for a week
or
wear a tuxedo to school for a month?

Would you rather

be a famous singer
or
a famous dancer?

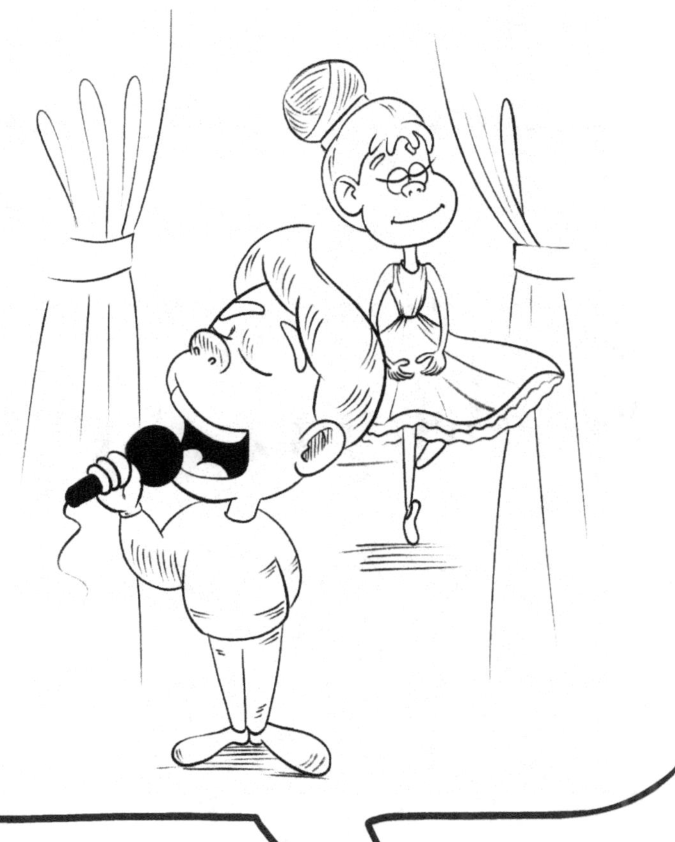

Would you rather

write an essay
or
do a science experiment?

Would you rather

have flowers for hair
or
vegetables for arms?

Would you rather

have a fire-breathing dragon as a pet
or
eat snails on your next five pizzas?

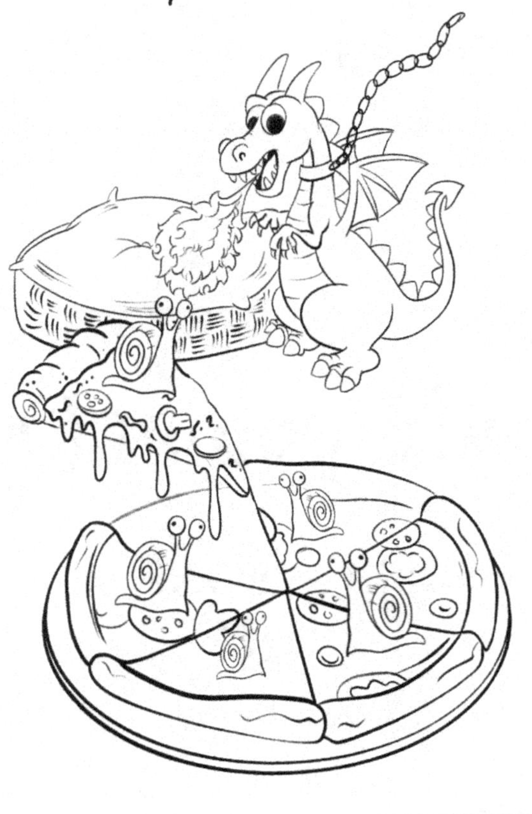

Would you rather

learn how to march with penguins in Antarctica

or

learn to eat bamboo with pandas in china?

Would you rather

control the weather

or

control the ocean?

Would you rather

have a magic mirror and twenty fingers
or
have a fairy godmother and twenty toes?

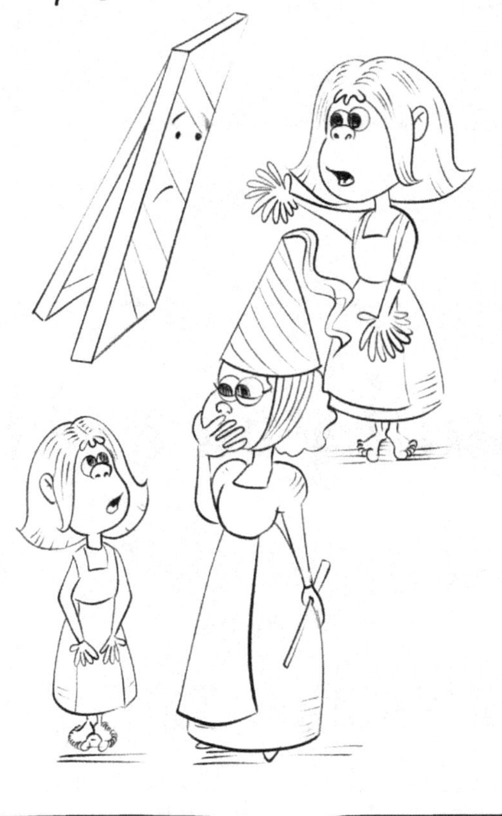

Would you rather

Sing everything you want to say
or
never be able to sing again?

Would you rather

live on a stranded island full of bunnies
or
live on a continent full of giraffes?

Would you rather

throw fireworks
or
confetti from your fingertips?

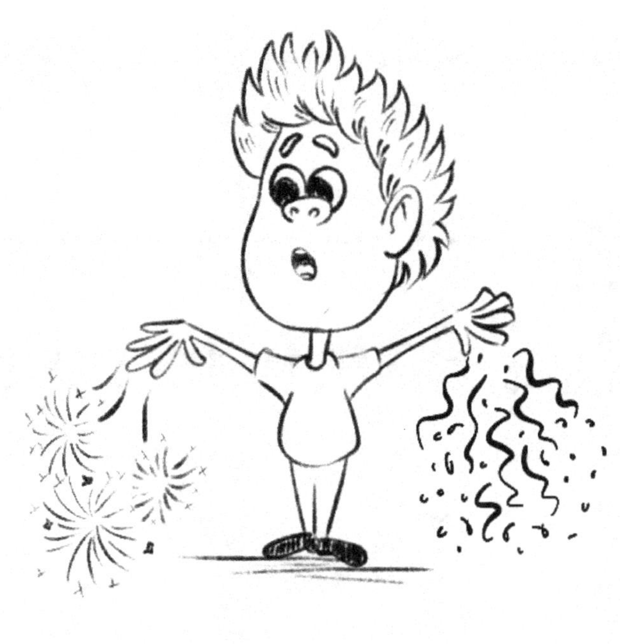

Would you rather

be a trapeze artist in a circus
or
be an elephant trainer in a circus?

Would you rather

rather be royalty
or
be a famous singer?

Would you rather

have a holiday named after you
or
have a planet named after you?

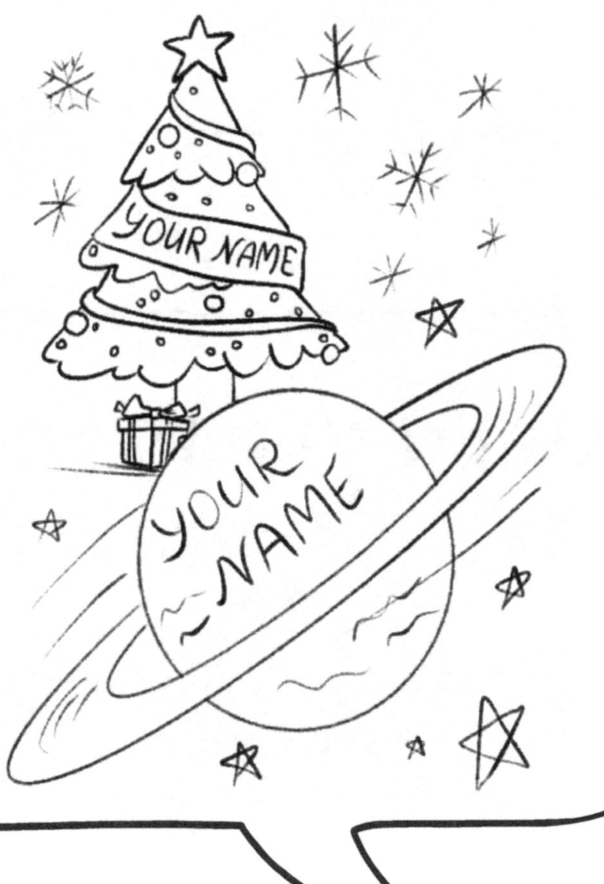

Would you rather

be able to see smells
or
hear colors?

Would you rather

live in one of Egypt's pyramids
or
go to school in the International
Space Station?

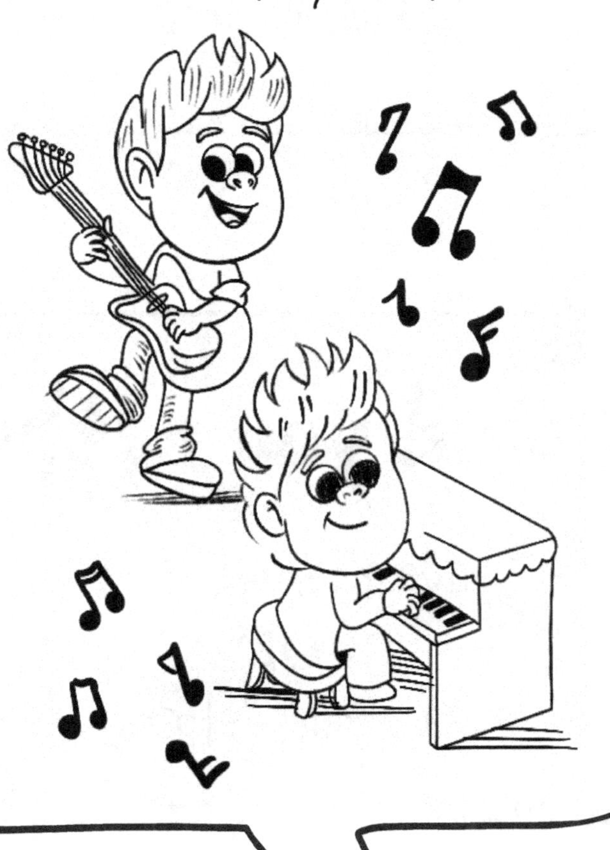

Would you rather

learn how to play guitar
or
learn how to play the piano?

Would you rather

eat a whole lemon
or
a whole onion?

Would you rather

have a personal robot
or
a personal jetpack?

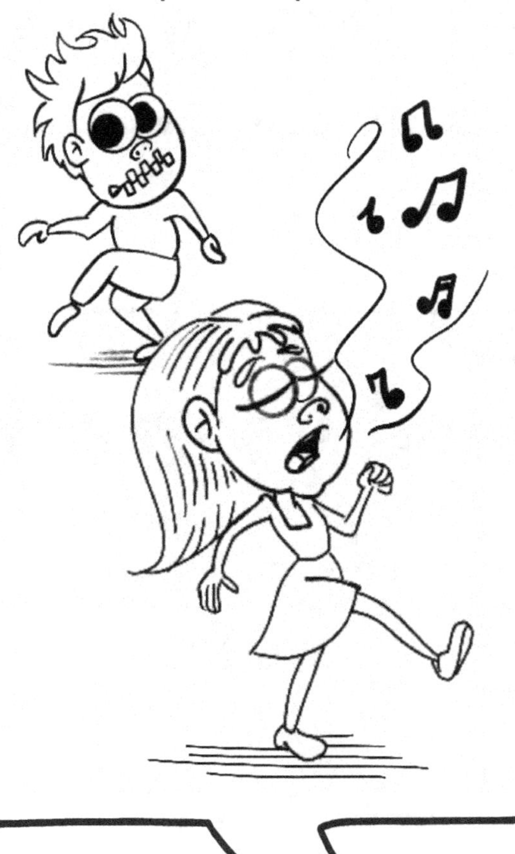

Would you rather
be able to move silently
or
sing every time you walk?

"Would you rather

have ten silly hats on your head at once
or
have ten silly hair bows on your head at once?"

"Would you rather

be in an art class
or
in a music class?"

Would you rather

meet aliens
or
meet talking octopi?

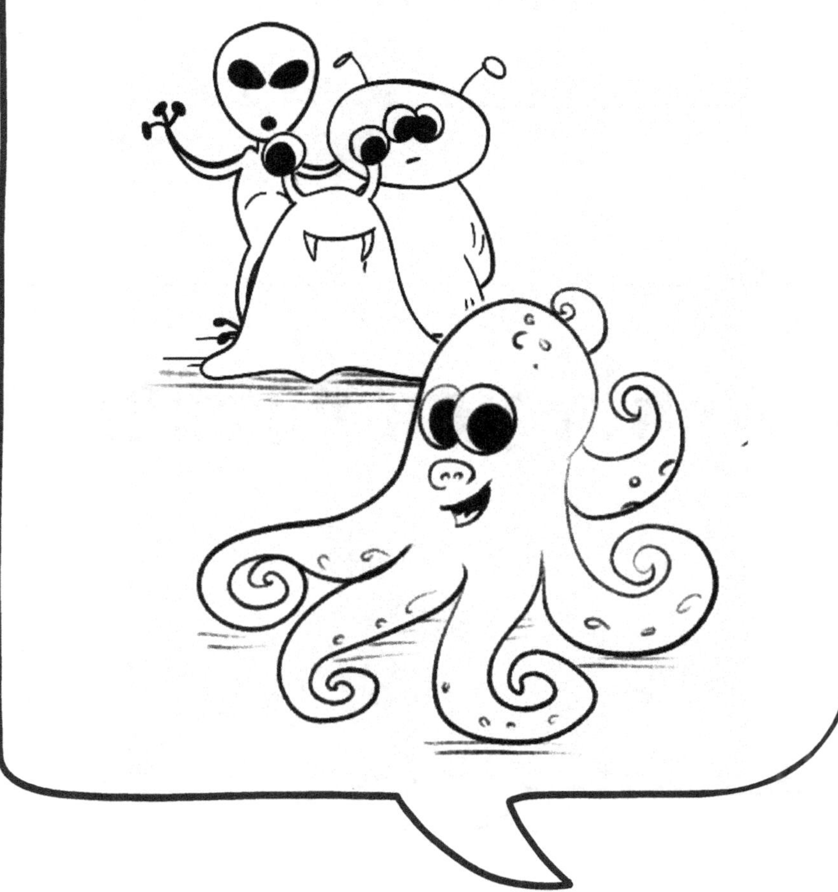

Would you rather

eat ten bananas
or
ten blueberries?

Would you rather

have three purple eyes
or
have two purple noses?

Would you rather

have a pet spider
or
a pet snake?

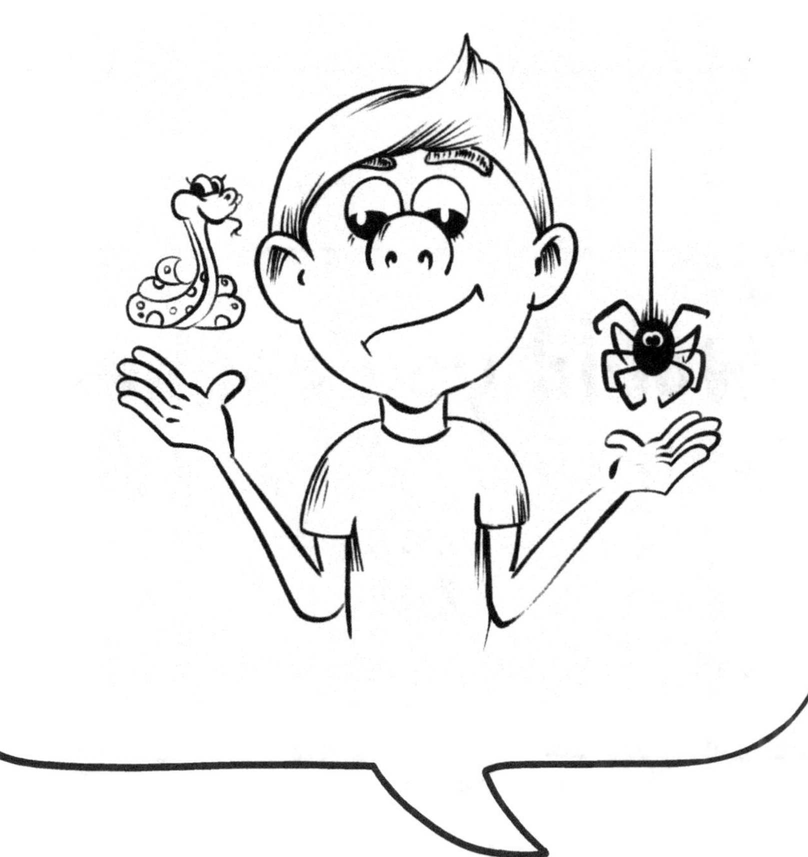

Would you rather

rather ride on a hot air balloon
or
ride an airboat?

Would you rather

be able to blow giant, building-sized
bubbles,
or
whistle so loud everyone could hear you?

Would you rather

speak another language
or
be able to speak to animals?

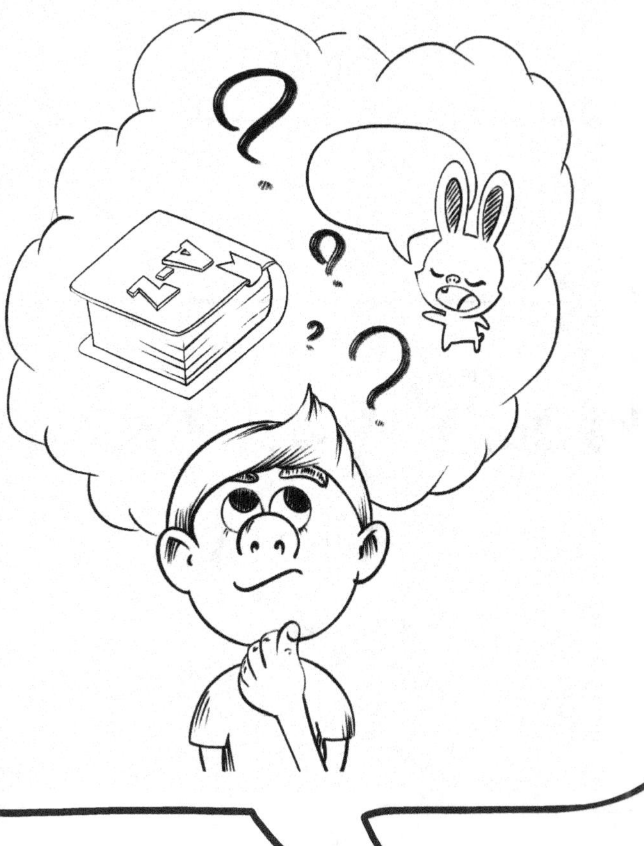

Would you rather

spend the day gardening with a talking spider

or

spend the day at a museum with a talking fly?

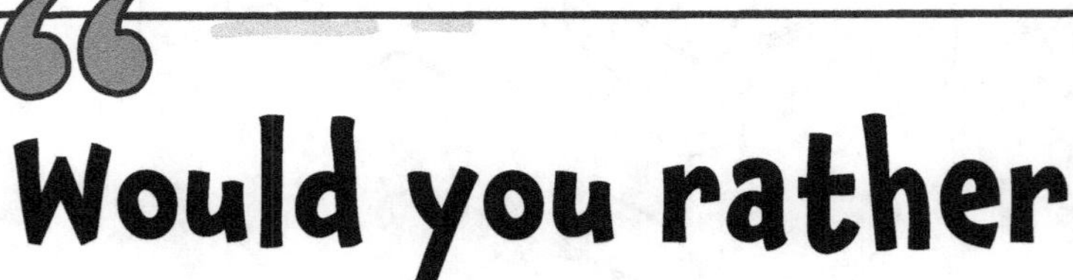

Would you rather

have a puppet show
or
watch your favorite movie?

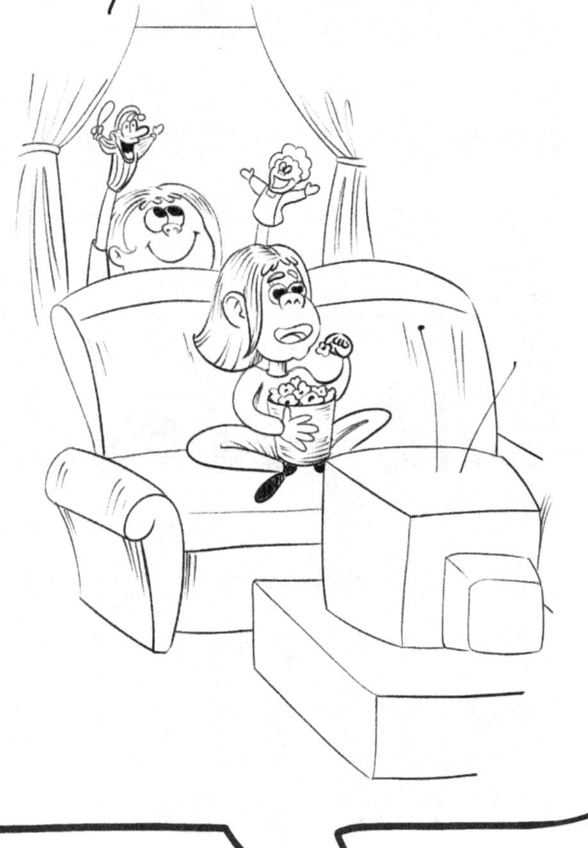

Would you rather
live in the jungle
or
live in the ocean?

Would you rather
spend a week at Disney World
or
spend a week at Seaworld?

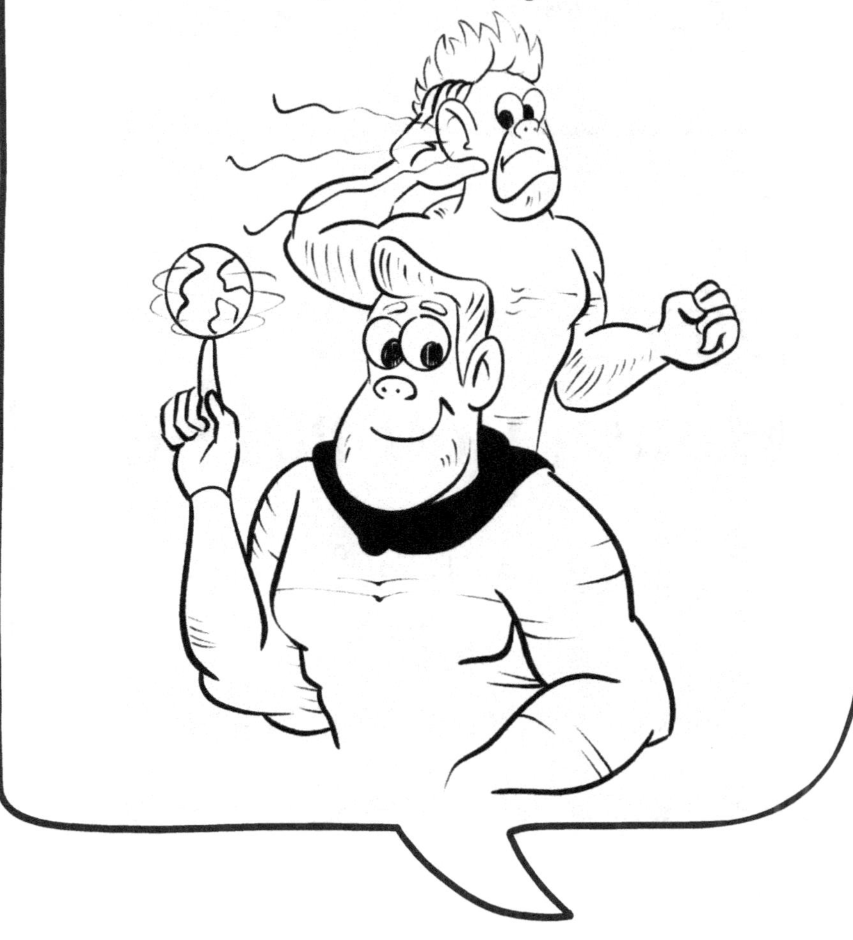

Would you rather
have super strength
or
super hearing?

Would you rather

be a photographer for wild animals
or
be a photographer for musicians?

Would you rather

sneeze ten times in a row
or
have the hiccups for an hour?

Would you rather

play video games with a kangaroo
or
play hide and see with a sloth?

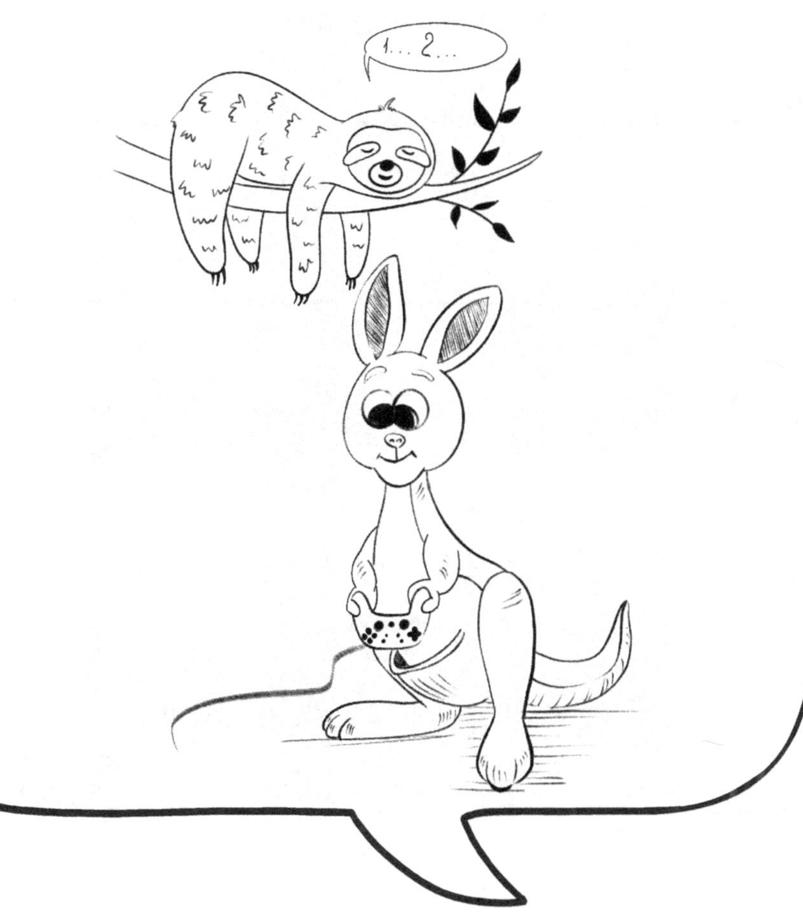

Would you rather

live in an old castle
or
live in an old airport?

Would you rather

go to a science center
or
go to a trampoline museum?

Would you rather

Sneeze Sugar
or
Sneeze cupcake Sprinkles?

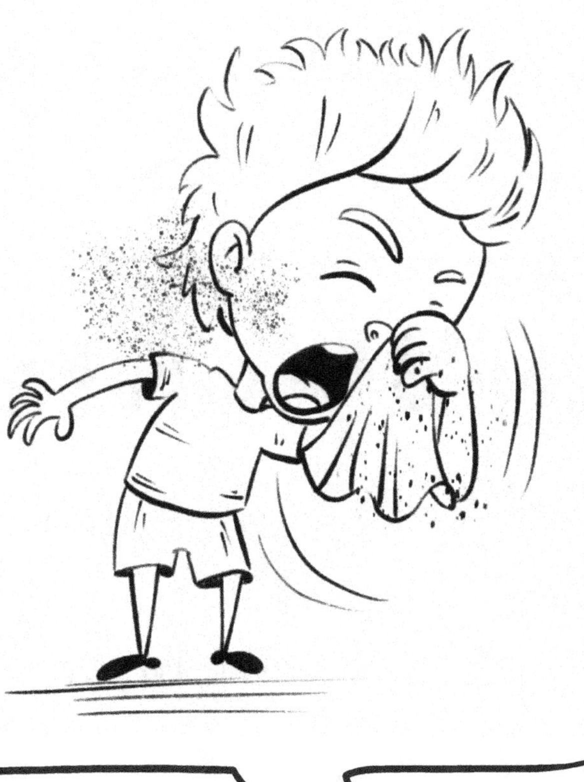

Would you rather

be a mermaid with black hair
or
be a pirate with pink hair?

Would you rather

the sky rained meatballs
or
drops of peanut butter?

Would you rather
raise a colony of ants under your bed
or
raise a pet penguin in your closet?

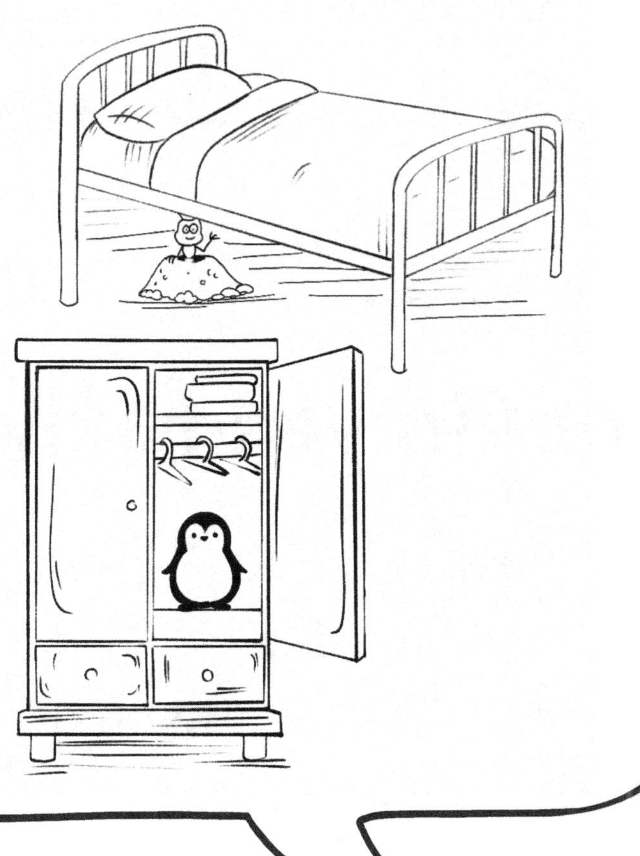

Would you rather

have pancakes for a pillow
or
have pancakes for a blanket?

Would you rather

read your favorite book
or
watch your favorite movie?

Would you rather

go camping
or
vacation in a beach-side hotel?

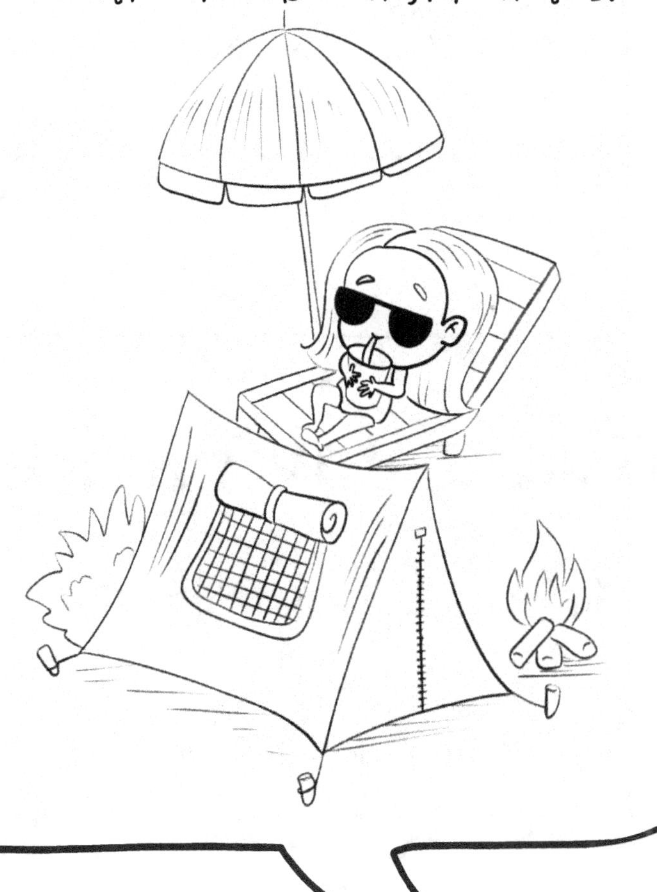

See into the future
or
visit the past?

Surf on waves of cotton candy
or
swim in an ocean of Nutella?

Would you rather

have a house made of S'mores
or
have a car made of cheese?

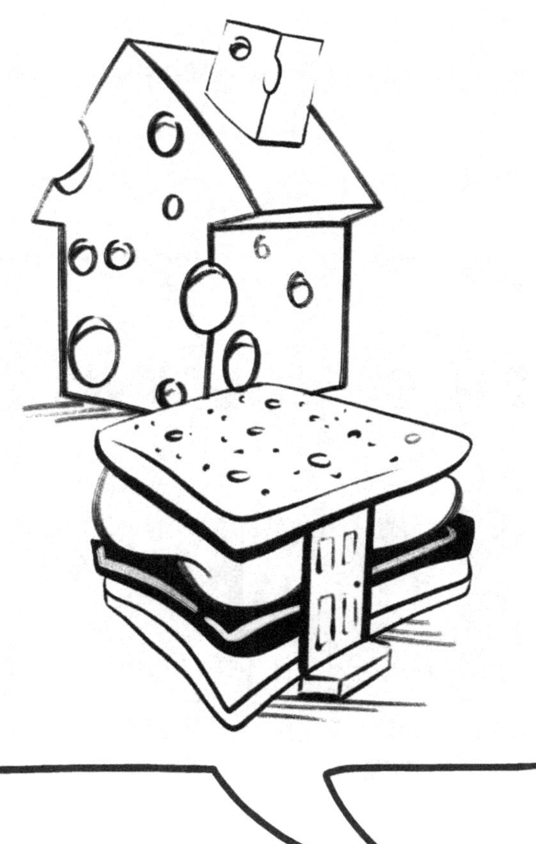

Would you rather

shower in JELL-O
or
bathe in donuts?

Would you rather

have a pie smooshed into your face
or
get dunked in ice cold water?

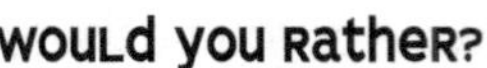

Would you rather

have super speed
or
have night vision?

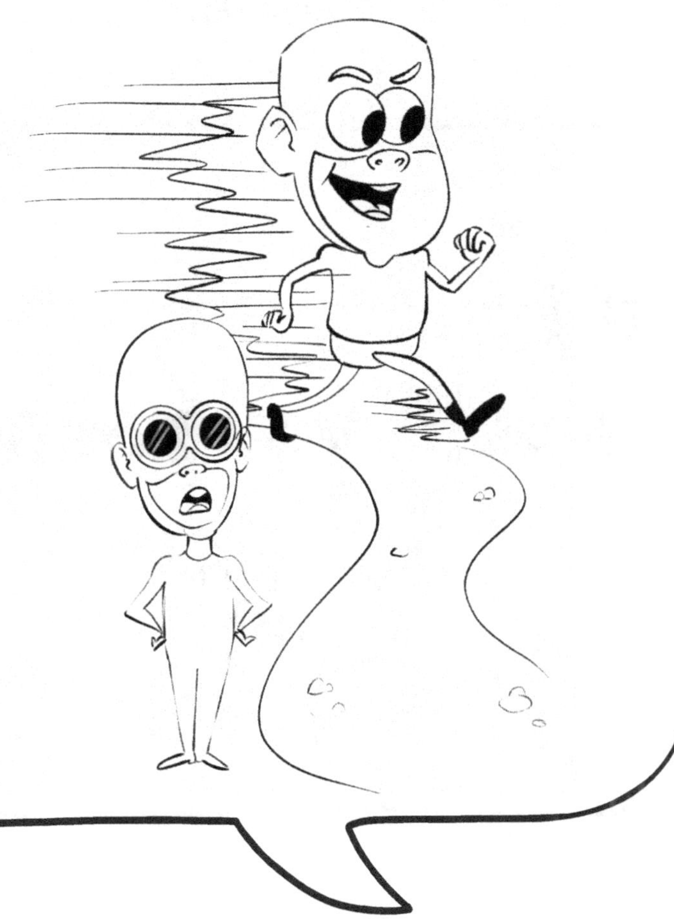

Would you rather
be BATMAN
or
Superman?

Would you rather
be catwoman
or
Superwoman?

Would you rather

live on a farm with cows and chickens
or
live in a big city with trains and buses?

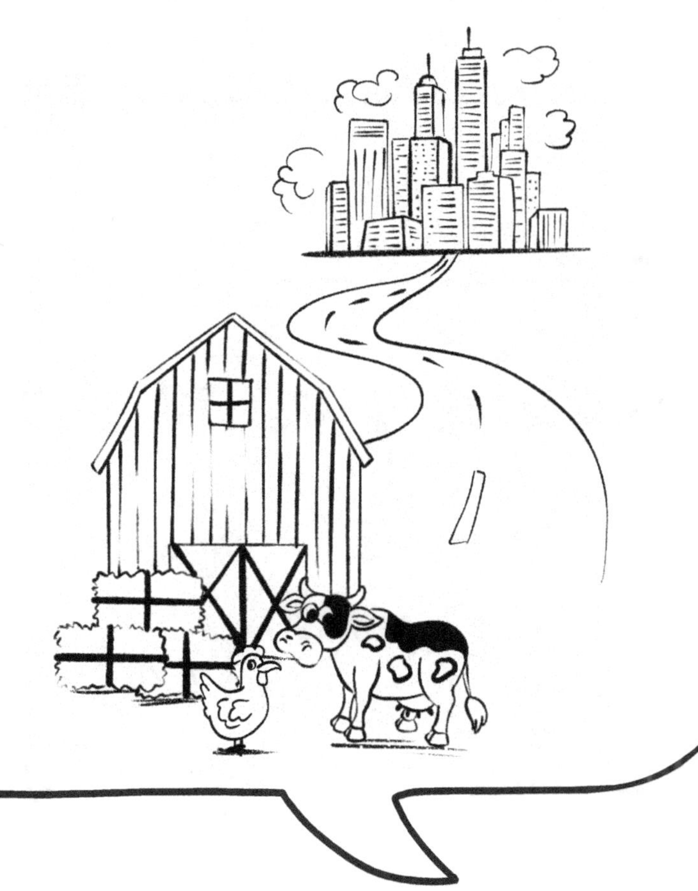

Would you rather

have a school uniform
or
wear whatever you want?

Would you rather

have a star in your closet
or
visit another solar system?

Would you rather

eat skittles
or
eat PB&J sandwiches for a week?

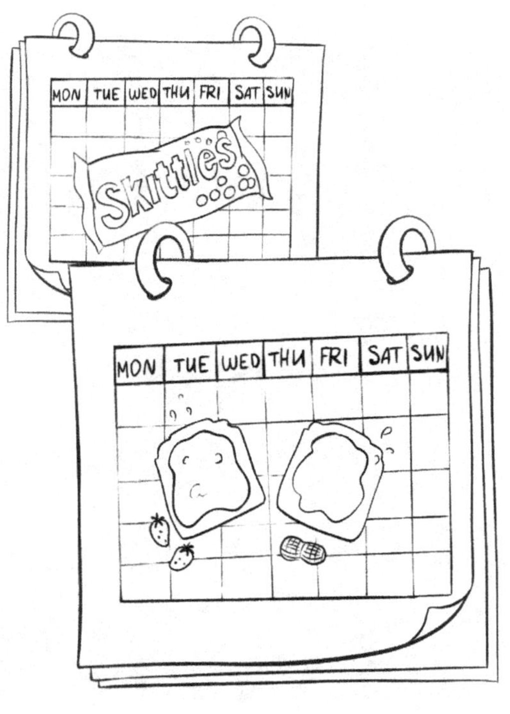

Would you rather

have the world's largest gummy bear
or
the world's largest gummy worm?

Would you rather

visit the Grand Canyon
or
the Eiffel Tower?

Would you rather
be a princess **or**
be a swashbuckling pirate?

Would you rather

have a dance party at a roller rink

or

have a talent show at a bowling alley?

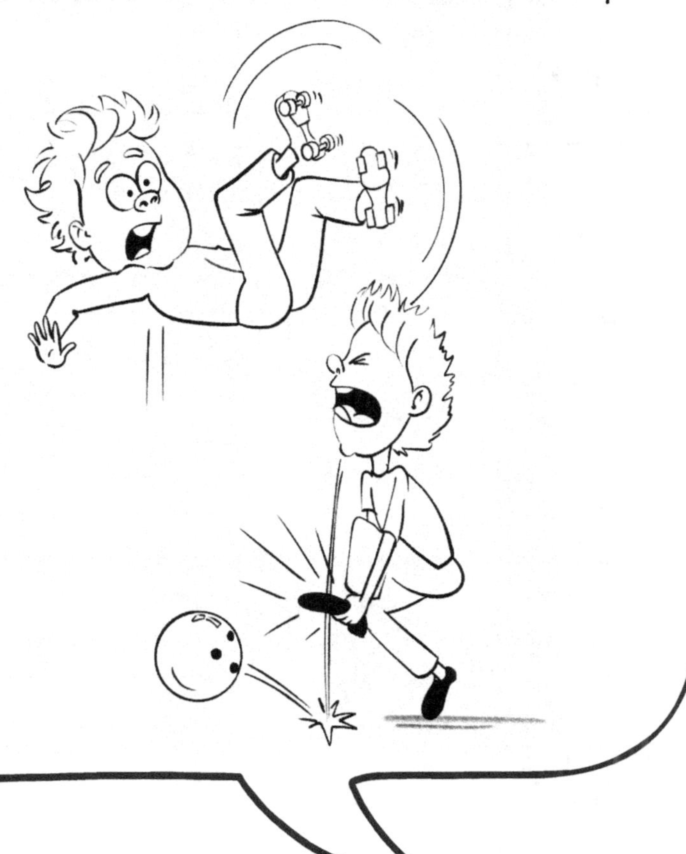

Chapter Two:
Jokes

Why didn't the teddy bear eat dessert?
o   Because he was stuffed.

What did the dad buffalo say on the first day of school?
o   "Bi-son!"

I'm great friends with 25 letters of the alphabet! I don't know "y."

A child is hiking one day with his family when he stumbles upon a lamp. He dusts the side of the lamp and a genie pops out. "What is your first wish?" The genie asks. The child excitedly says, "I wish I were rich!"
The genie nods. "Done. What's your next wish, Rich?"

Knock, knock!
    Who's there?
Leon!
    Leon, who?
Leon on me when you're not strong and I'll be your friend.

What did the giraffe say after dinner?
o   "That hit the spot!"

Being a doctor would be fun, but I don't think I'd have enough patients.

What does a computer eat for lunch?
o   A byte.

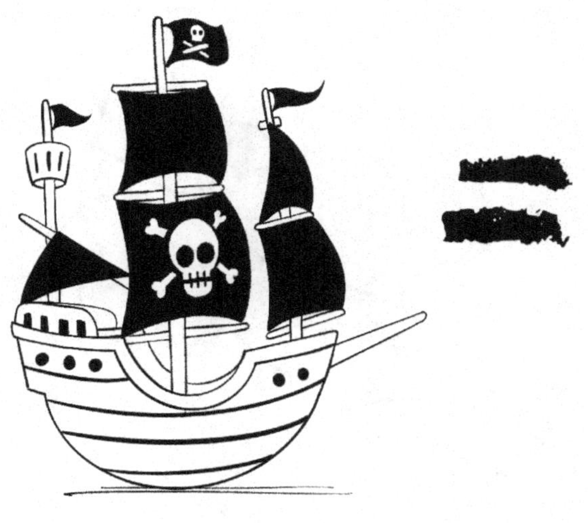

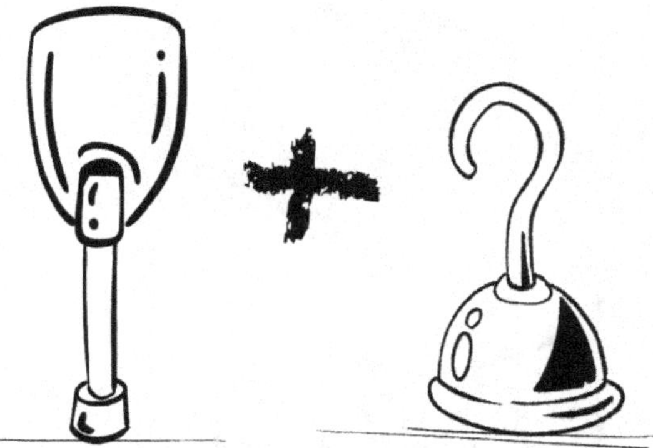

How much does it cost a pirate to get a ship?

An arm and a wooden leg!

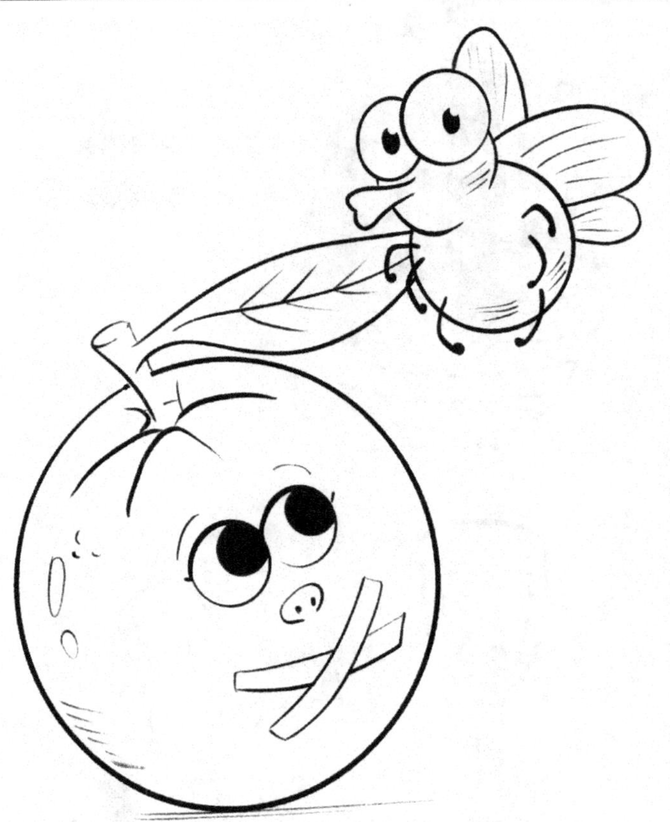

What did the orange say to the fly?

Nothing. Oranges don't talk.

A man walks into a restaurant and is seated at a table. After a few moments looking over the menu, he orders the soup of the day. Soon, a waiter brings the man his soup and sets it on the table.

"I can't eat this soup," the man says to the waiter. "Oh, is it too hot? Too cold?" The waiter asks. The man simply shakes his head. "No, no."

The waiter, confused, goes to get the chef and the restaurant manager. They proceed to ask the man if the soup is wrong, if it's too hot or cold, or if it isn't to his liking. "No, no, no." The man continues to answer. Slightly irritated, the chef furrows his brow. "I'll try and see what's wrong. Where's a spoon?"

"Exactly," says the man.

Knock, knock!
   Who's there?
Lena!
   Lena, who?
Lena little on the railing so you can get a better view!

What has ears but doesn't hear anything?
o   A bucket of corn!

I want to be an archaeologist, but I think my career would be in ruins.

Why are math books so sad?
o   They have so many problems.

Why did the clock get removed from the library?
o   It tock-ed too much!

Knock, knock!
   Who's there?
Wa!
   Wa, who?
What are you so excited about?

While at the grocery store, a customer accidentally drops a bag of flour all over the flour. An associate of the store comes with clean up materials and to work getting it all cleaned up. "Don't bother, young man. It's self-rising!"

What is loud, crunchy, and hot?
o   A rocket chip!

I tried making a pencil that had an eraser on two ends, but there would be no point.

What is hairy, brown, and wears sunscreen?
o   A coconut on the beach.

Where do skateboarders go to school?
o   Boarding school!

Kid: What are you doing under there?
Mom: Under where?
Kid: Made you say underwear!

What kind of tree belongs in your hand?
o   A palm tree.

Why did the cookie go to the clinic?
o   Because he felt crumbly.

Knock, knock!
    Who's there?
Dewey!
    Dewey, who?
Dewey still have to go to school?

Why did the student study on a plane?
o   To get higher education!

Two kids sign up to go to a haunted house in a forest for the local Halloween festivities. The local guide tells them that since it's in the forest, they might see some animals wandering through. Sure enough, a panda wanders in front of them as they explore. Both kids scream and run away.

"What happened?" The local guide frantically asks as they run out.

"We saw a panda ghost!" One boy exclaims.

"How do you know it was a ghost?" The guide asks.

"It was eating bam-boooo!"

Knock, knock!
Who's there?
I am!
I am, who?
You don't know who you are?!

What animal loves to watch baseball?
o   A bat.

A man walked into a bar. Ouch!

Knock, knock!
Who's there?
Quiche!
Quiche, who?
Can I have a hug and a quiche?

Why is it so hard for pirates to learn to spell?
o   They get lost at c.

What falls during the autumn but doesn't get hurt?
o   Leaves!

What do you call a ghost's first love?
o   His soulmate.

A man goes to a lawyer and asks about his fees.
"I charge $100 for three questions," the lawyer says.
"That's pretty steep, isn't it?" The man asks.
"Yes, it can be expensive." The lawyer says. "Now, what is your last question?"

I used to do the hokey pokey too much. Thankfully, I've turned myself around.

Why didn't the fish go on vacation?
o   It was too busy in school!

What did the volcano say to the other volcano?
o   "Lava me alone!"

Knock, knock!
   Who's there?
Hike!
   Hike, who?
I didn't know you were a fan of Japanese poetry!

How does the moon become a hairdresser?
o   Eclipse hair.

How do you make friends with a squirrel?
o   You act nutty!

I saw Cinderella at baseball tryouts, but she kept running away from the ball.

A handyman goes door to door to look for work. One of the homeowners he talks to says he'll pay $150 for the handyman to paint his porch. The handyman agrees and gets to work. A few hours later, the handyman comes to the homeowner to let him know how it is going. "I'm all done, but you should know that your car is a Ferrari, not a Porsche."

What did the colored pencils say to each other?
o   "You're looking so sharp!"

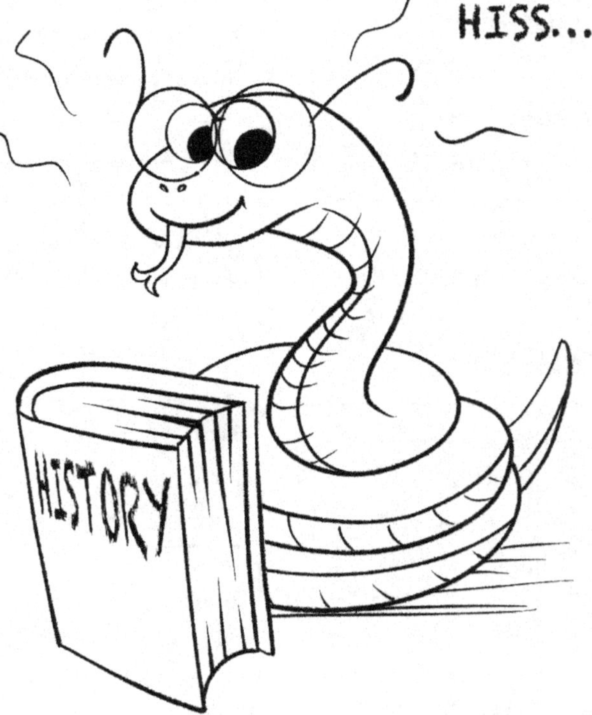

What is a snake's favorite school subject?

Hiss-tory!

Knock, knock!
Who's there?
Just an old lady. Little old lady too.
A little old lady too, who?
Wow! I didn't know you were able to yodel so well!

What does a vampire with a cold do?
o   It keeps coffin!

I tried to remember which direction the sun rises in the morning, but then it dawned on me.

What do spiders love to do for a living?
o   Web design!

I've had amnesia for as long as I...

What do stars and fake teeth have in common?
o   They both come out at night.

Knock, knock!
Who's there?
Ice cream soda!
Ice cream soda, who?
Ice cream soda people can hear me over the crowds!

Why do calendars make great best friends?
o   You can always rely on them.

Birds don't usually make puns, but toucan!

What do scientists use to keep their breath fresh?
o   Experi-mints!

What has five eyes and loves the water?
o   The Mississippi River!

Knock, knock!
Who's there?
Haven!
Haven, who?
Haven you heard enough knock-knock jokes yet?

I finished this puzzle in a month, but the box said it would take 9+ years.

What type of library has books of all one color?
o   One where all the books are red.

How is a pickle born?
o   From a jarring experience.

What does a computer have when it's sick?
o   A computer virus.

Knock, knock!
    Who's there?
Double!
    Double, who?
W!

What is the music teacher's favorite place to vacation?
o   The Florida Keys!

What do you call a boomerang that doesn't come back to you?
o   A curved stick.

Teacher: Why are you so late?
Student: I ate my alarm clock this morning. It was very time-consuming.

Why did the T-Rex cross the road?
o   Because they hadn't become chickens yet.

How do you make tissues dance?
o   You put some boogie in them!

Leopards are great at hide-and-seek, but they always get spotted!

Why didn't Elsa get a balloon?
o Because she would let it go.

Knock, knock!
Who's there?
Spell!
Spell, who?
W-H-O!

How do you get an octopus to laugh?
o By ten-tickling him!

Knock, knock!
Whos' there?
Nobel.
Nobel, who?
There's no bell, that's why I knocked!

What did the nose yell at the fingers?
o "Don't be picky!"

What instrument can you play at the bathroom sink?
o A tuba-toothpaste!

Knock, knock!
Whos' there?
Tank.
Tank, who?
You're welcome!

Why did Timmy bring a ladder to school?
o Because he was ready for high school!

How are cupcakes and baseball similar?
o They both need some batter!

What gets more wet as it dries?
o Towels!

Knock, knock!
Whos' there?
Cow says.
Cow says, who?
No, no, a cow says moo.

Where do vampires use the ATM?
o At a blood bank.

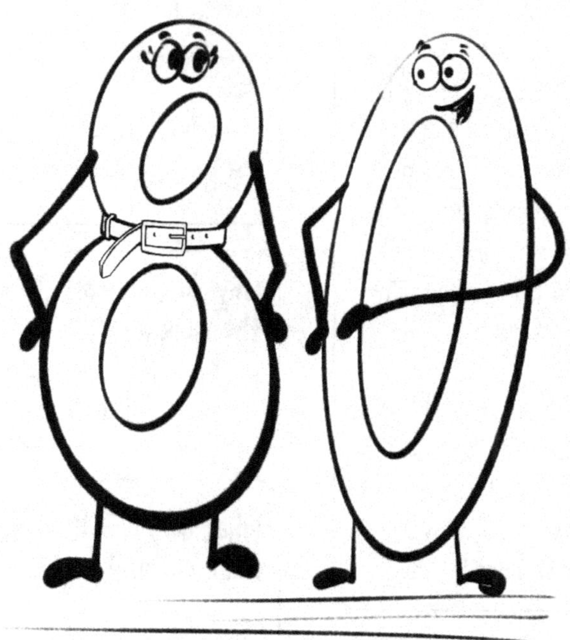

What did 0 say to 8?

Nice belt

Three friends are stranded on a deserted island when they stumble upon a magic lamp. They rub the lamp and a genie pops out. "Usually, I give the person who finds me three wishes, but since there are three of you, you can each get a single wish." The first friend cries tears of joy. "I want to go home!" The genie grants her wish. "I want to go home, too!" The second friend says. The genie grants her wish as well.

When the genie asks the third friend, she frowns. "I'm lonely," the third friend says. "I wish my friends were here."

What do cake and dishes have in common?
o   They can be spongy!

Knock, knock!
    Who's there?
Deja!
    Deja, who?
Knock, knock!

What's the best vacation destination for a pack of pencils?
o   Pencil-vania!

Knock, knock!
    Whos' there?
Hawaii.
    Hawaii, who?
I'm good, Hawaii you?

Why do they call the past the Dark Ages?
o   Because there were too many knights!

What do you call noodles made of cardboard?
o   Impasta!

Why did the orange see a doctor?
o   Because he wasn't peeling well.

Kid1: Someone in here is an owl.
Kid2: Who?
Kid1, gasping: It's you!

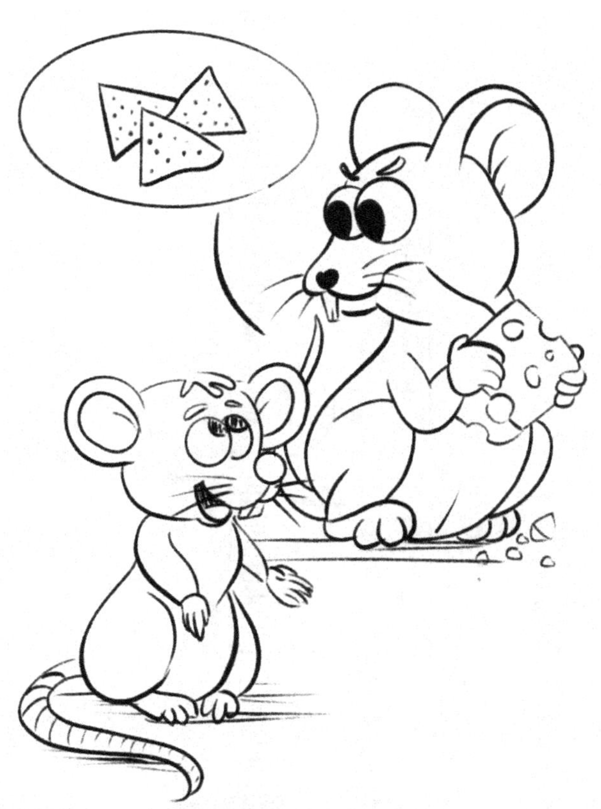

What did the mouse say
when another mouse
tried to take his cheese?

"That's nacho cheese!"

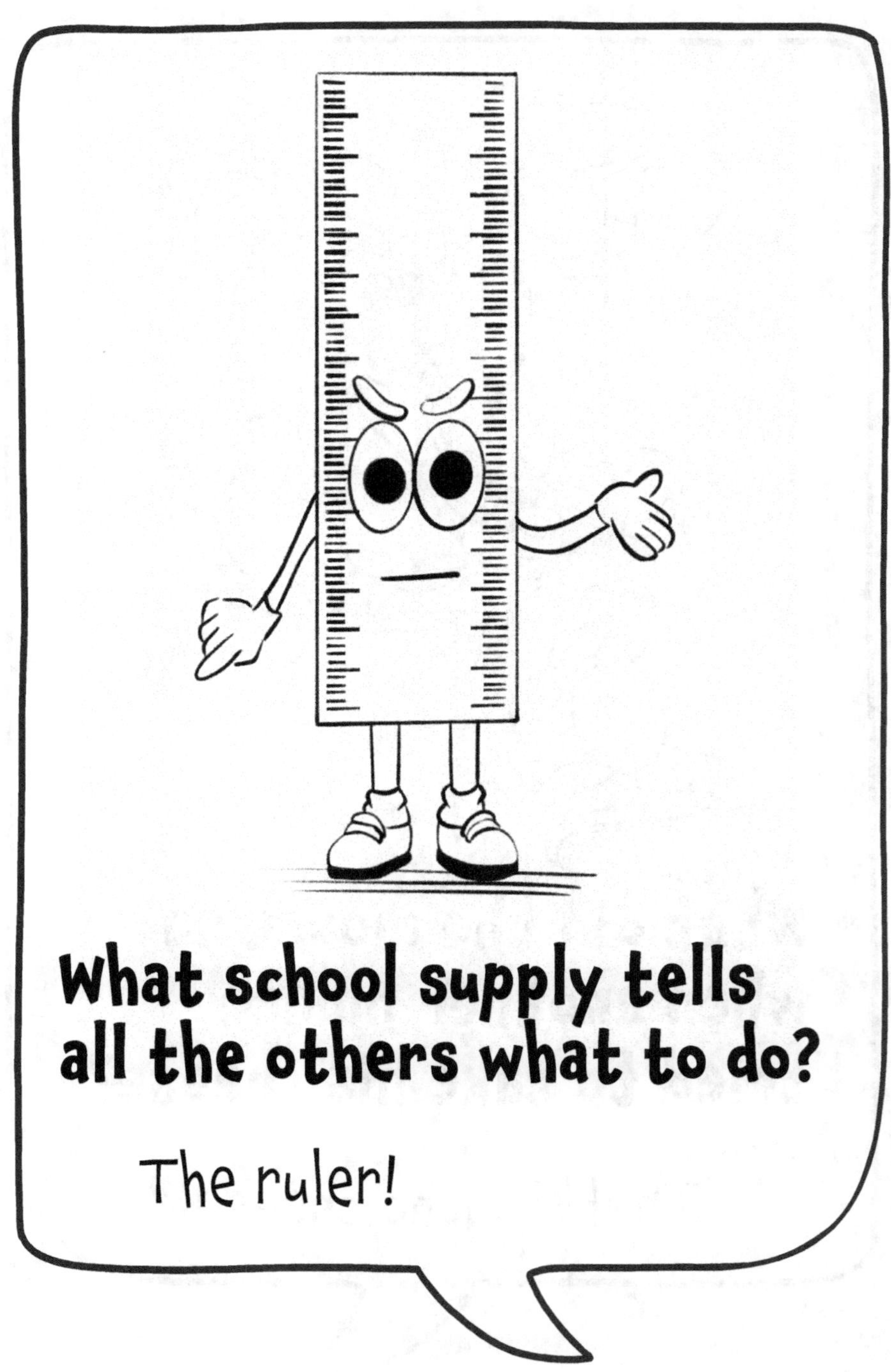

What school supply tells
all the others what to do?

The ruler!

What is a frog's favorite game?
o Hopscotch.

How did vikings talk to each other?
o Norse code!

What stays in a corner and sees the world?
o A stamp!

What subject would a witch teach in school?
o Spelling!

What award did the dentist win?
o A plaque of achievement.

What is a math teacher's favorite season of the year?
o Sum-mer!

What do you call mountains that make you laugh?
o Hill-arious!

Knock, knock!
  Whos' there?
Water.
  Water, who?
Water you doing telling jokes, we need to get to class!

What did the dad flower say to his son?
o "Hey, bud!"

Knock, knock!
  Who's there?
Owl says!
  Owl says, who?
That's very true, they do.

If at first you don't succeed, skydiving is not the career for you.

Why did the teacher have to wear sunglasses to class?
o Because her pupils were so bright!

Why are ghosts bad at lying?
o   You can see through them!

Where do fish store cash?
o   On a riverbank!
Knock, knock!
    Whos' there?
Canoe.
    Canoe, who?
Canoe open the door for me!

Why did an invisible man turn down a career?
o   He couldn't see himself being happy with it.

How did the computer catch a cold?
o   He left the windows open!

I just made a song about a burrito, but it's more of a rap.

What did the student say when the teacher asked if the student missed school?
o   "Not at all!"

Who cleans the ocean?
o   Mer-maids.
Knock, knock!
    Who's there?
Beats!
    Beats, who?
Beats me!

Why did the new principal jump in the lake?
o   To test the waters!

Knock, knock!
    Whos' there?
Iran.
    Iran, who?
Iran here! I'm so tired!

Which dinosaur was the best writer?
o   The thesaurus!

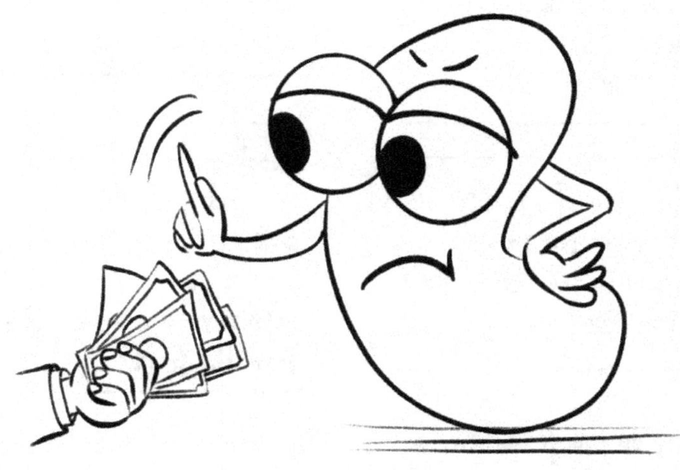

Which nut doesn't like money?
Cash-ew

What did the ghost teacher say to his class?

o "Open your booo-ks to page 25."

Why did the apple lose a race?

o He ran out of juice.

I think I want to be an electrician, but I think everyone would be shocked by how good I am.

What do you get when you toss books into the ocean?

o A title wave!

Knock, knock!
    Who's there?
Opportunity!
    Opportunity, who?
Opportunity doesn't knock twice!

Why are rhinos bad dancers?

o Rhinos have two left feet!

What did the sink say to the toilet?

o "You look flushed."

How do you have a party in outer space?

o You have to planet.

Knock, knock!
    Whos' there?
Dose.
    Dose, who?
Dose anyone want anything from the store?

Why did the banana throw the clock out the window?

o To see time fly!

What is a sleeping bull called?

o A bulldozer!

I tried to explain to my little sister that sometimes it's okay to poop your pants, but she's still laughing at me.

What do you call a caterpillar and a parrot having a picnic?
o   A walkie talkie.

Why didn't the motorcycle stand up?
o   It was two-tired!

Why don't robots have any fear?
o   Their nerves are made of steel.

Two pickles fell out of the jar, but they just had to Dill with it.

What letter do pirates like most?
o   Arrr.

Why was the tomato blushing on the cutting board?
o   Because he saw salad dressing!

Why did the man take his clock to the doctor?
o   He was afraid it had too many ticks!

What kind of egg does an evil hen lay?
o   A deviled egg.

Knock, knock!
    Whos' there?
Olive.
    Olive, who?
Olive you more!

What type of bus crosses the ocean?
o   A Columbus!

What kind of clothes do books wear in winter?
o   Jackets!

What sound does a giant cowbell make?
o   A cow-boom.

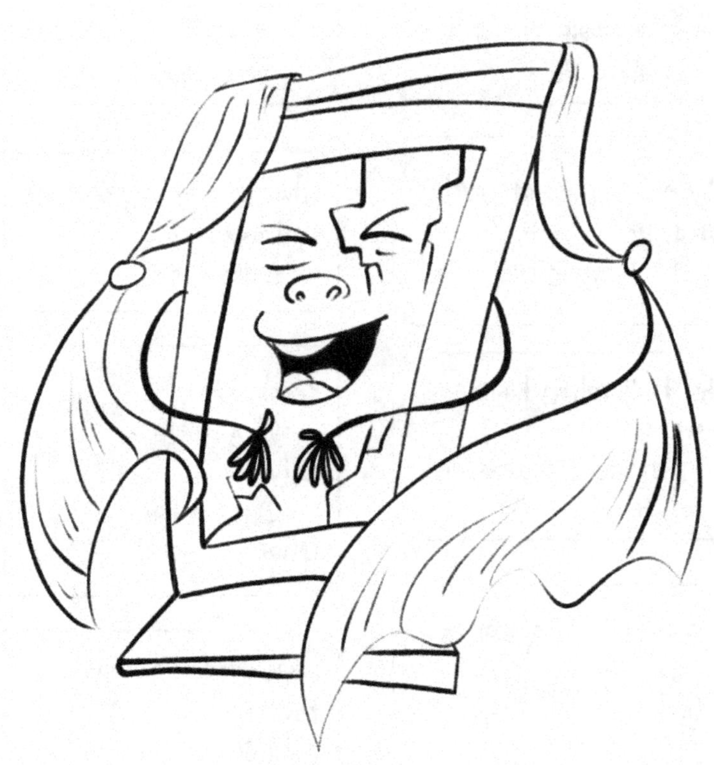

Why shouldn't you tell
great jokes near windows?

They would crack up!

What hairstyle do wasps
like most?
o   Buzzcuts!

Knock, knock!
    Who's there?
Amish!
    Amish, who?
you're a shoe? um, okay.

When a T-Rex sleeps, all you
can hear is its dino-snore!

What has legs but doesn't
walk?
o   Pants!

What has four legs but
doesn't walk?
o   A table.

Knock, knock!
    Who's there?
Dough-nut!
    Dough-nut, who?
I dough-nut know, ask
someone else!

How do you get peanut
butter off a door handle?
o   you use a door jam.

Why can't you have a
sleepover with pigs?
o   They always hog the
    blankets!

Why is it so hard to play
games with porcupines?
o   They always have the
    most points.

What vegetable can break a
dishwasher?
o   A leek.

The picture was in jail,
but it turned out he was
framed!

What would you call a pig
who has mastered karate?
o   A pork chop!

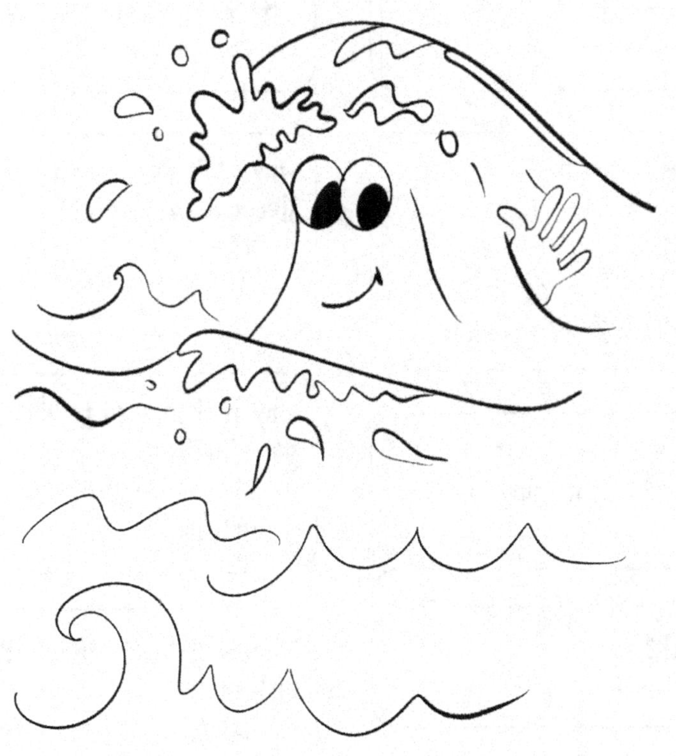

How does the sea act friendly?

It waves.

Where do elephants store their clothes on a road trip?
o   In their trunk!

Why was the hair running late?
o   It was over-swept!

What is a loaf of bread's favorite vacation activity?
o   Toasting in the sun.

What is a loaf of bread's favorite vacation activity?
o   Toasting in the sun.

There is a woman traveling with her baby on a train when a man sits next to her. He gasps and points to her baby. "Ma'am, that is the ugliest baby I've ever seen. You should get him checked out as soon as possible." Furious, the woman shouts for the conductor. "Conductor, this man has insulted me! I demand a new seat!"

What medicine does a sick lemon need?
o   Lemon-aide!

There are two muffins baking in the oven. One of the muffins turns to the other and says, "Boy, is it hot in here." The other muffin gasps, "Oh my god! A talking muffin!"

"I'm so sorry about this, ma'am," the conductor says. "This is absolutely unacceptable. I'll handle him later, but for you, please come to the nicer first-class seats, and we'll get a complimentary banana for your monkey."

Knock, knock!
    Whos' there?
Ice cream.
    Ice cream, who?
It's cold! Ice cream if you don't open the door!

Why did the scarecrow get a promotion?
o He was outstanding in his field!

Where does the president keep his armies?
o In his sleevies.

What is a cow's favorite activity?
o Going to the mooo-vies.

How do you weigh a fish?
o Use scales!

A man and his daughter walk into a library and go to the front desk. To the librarian, the man says, "I'll have a cheeseburger and French fries, please."

The librarian raises an eyebrow. "Sir, this is a library."

"Oh, I'm sorry." The man says. Whispering, he leans forward. "I'll have a cheeseburger and French fries, please."

What is a ghost's favorite snack?
o Boo-mpkin pie!

Why did the bank robber hose down his money?
o He wanted a clean getaway!

Frogs are so happy because they eat whatever bugs them.

What did the berry bushes say to the harvesting machine?
o "Don't pick on me!"

What fruit do ghosts love the most?
o Boo-berries.

What dies but never really lives?
o A remote control.

Why was it so hard for the ghost to visit his parents?
o   Because they were transparent

A boy and his father are sitting at the dinner table one night when the boy asks, "Dad, are bugs good to eat?"

The father frowns. "That's gross to talk about while eating. We'll talk about bugs later."

Later, after dinner is finished, the father goes to his son. "What was your question about bugs?"

"Oh, nothing," his son replies. "There was a bug in your mashed potatoes, but it's gone now."

Knock, knock!
    Whos' there?
Boo.
    Boo, who?
Aw, don't cry! It was just a joke.

What would you call Dracula's fans?
o   A fang club.

What did one eye say to the other eye?
o   Don't look or anything but something between us smells.

Why did the cyclops quit teaching?
o   He could only see one pupil at a time.

Why did the computer go to see a dentist?
o   It had Bluetooth!

Why don't vampires make friends easily?
o   They are usually pains in the neck.

What type of underwear does Thor have?
o   Thunderwear!

I'd pamper my pet cow but then she'd just give me spoiled milk.

What kind of games do kids have to play when the electricity goes out in a storm?
o   Bored games!

What is a spider's favorite event?
o   A webbing!

How can you tell when a car is thinking really hard?
o   You'll see its wheels spinning.

Knock, knock!
    Whos' there?
Theodore.
    Theodore, who?
Theodore is stuck! Get some help!

What did Benjamin Franklin say when he discovered electricity?
o   "I'm shocked!"

What shoes do thieves wear?
o   Sneakers.

How do posters talk to each other all day?
o   They use sign language.

How are a guitar and a fish different?
o   You can tune guitars but you can't tuna fish.

What kind of music do elves like the most?
o   Wrap music.

Why was the stadium so windy?
o   There were too many fans.

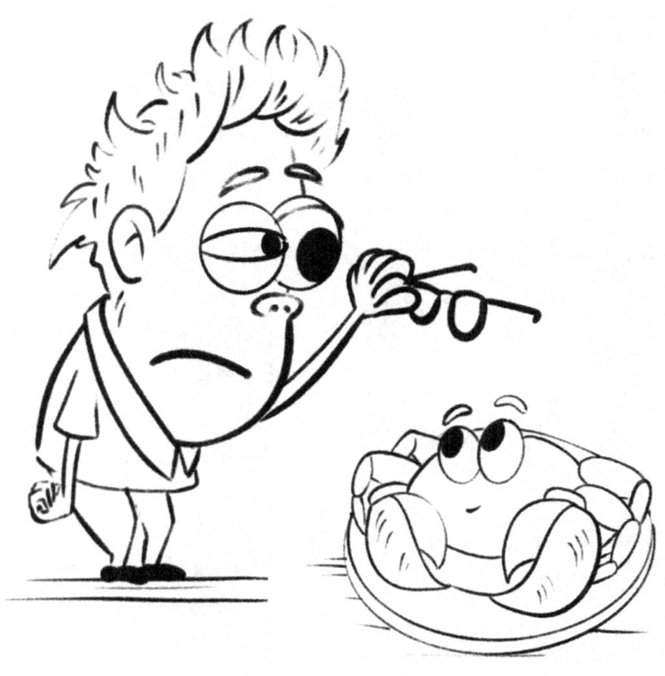

I'm on a strict seafood diet: I see food and I eat it.

Why was the lamp floating in the lake?

o   Because it was so light.

A detective and his assistant decide to go camping one night. They pitch their tent under the clear, starlit sky and head to sleep inside it.

Sometime during the night, the detective wakes his assistant and says, "Look up at the sky and tell me what you're seeing!"

The assistant says, "I see millions of stars."

"And, what does it mean?" The detective asks.

"Well, if there are millions of stars, there are probably millions of planets, which means there are probably other forms of life out there." The assistant looks at the detective.

The detective nods and shrugs. "I don't know. To me, it looks like somebody stole our tent."

It's so wet in England because the Queen has reigned there for decades.

Why should you whisper in a cornfield?

o   Because there are so many ears.

What do snowmen always smell?

o   Carrots!

What did the fisherman say when he was practicing magic tricks?

o   "Pick a cod, any cod!"

Why did the golfer bring an extra sweater?

o   In case he got a hole in one.

Conclusion

That's it! Now, you've learned how to play the game Would you Rather and learned a lot of funny jokes and puns to take with you. Don't forget the "knock, knock" jokes, too! You can impress your friends and family members with all your funny remarks and your silly jokes for Would you Rather!

What have you learned about yourself and others? Are more people interested in living in an old castle or an old airport? Have your friends and family members heard any of your new, random puns?

You've probably learned a lot about who other people are and how you can keep them laughing. Maybe it's time for you to come up with your own Would you Rather questions and your own funny jokes! It's not too hard; simply ask yourself what you would rather do in even the craziest of situations. Anything is a joke if it makes you laugh (and is safe, of course)!

The best part of it all is that you can ask anything! It doesn't have to make a lot of sense or be possible at all. Instead, it can be the silliest, craziest thing you've ever heard that could never possibly happen — like having a spaceship made of banana peels and a crew of monkeys! Use your imagination and ask whatever your heart desires!

Now that you've learned how, you're on the right track for fun anytime, anywhere. Have fun learning all about yourself and your friends as you play with these questions. Laugh your heart out!

Now, get out there and enjoy!